ROAD NORTH

Tales of an Urban Sourdough

by William E. Chisham

The Road North - Tales of An Urban Sourdough

Published By:
Old Red Barn Publishing
P.O. Box 921
Sequim, WA 98382, USA

Produced in the United States of America

Soft cover ISBN: 0-615-13745-51995

Also by the Author

"Reflexions,": 1985-86
A Poetry Chapbook
1986

"The Photo Op"
2008

"Habitatin For Humanity"
2008

Dedication

This book is dedicated to John and Kate and their journeys, to my special Alaska friends, and to my wife, Kay, who walked into my life as I was enjoying an Alaska sunset from the foredeck of my boat home at Aurora Basin in Juneau. Also to the many friends, co-workers, and others I met during my fifteen years in Alaska.

Table of Contents

HOME IN ALASKA

Sometimes my damp chilly thoughts roam
About why people make Alaska their home
Midst cold Arctic winds that loudly howl
Making even the stoutest soul cry foul
As days of pelting icy vertical rain
Work to numb the innards of the brain
While short winter days and long nights
Drain folks of will to continue the fights
Against days of sinking into endless snow
That end with rivers of ice and mud in flow
Till at last the spring break-up fest
Lures the cabin-bound out of their nest
To join white sox and no-seeum critters
That delight in annoying outdoor sitters.
All this makes survival a real chore
Without much time to enjoy life anymore.
Then comes the glimpse that you seek
Of distant snow-covered mountain peak
Or a sunset up the channel as interlude,
After hiking trail silence and solitude,
Sights of bear and deer or sometimes a whale
And thereby hangs the real Alaska tale
Of why so many of us have come to stay
And wouldn't have it any other way.

Bill Chisham - 1990

THE ROAD NORTH

PROLOGUE

My journey North actually started twenty years before I finally arrived in Alaska. An insurance claims adjusting company that employed me in Northern California announced openings in their Alaska branch offices. This raised visions in my mind of life under more basic conditions than I had always been accustomed to. Perhaps the company-provided Mercury Comet would be replaced by a team of sled dogs as I headed to work from a remote log cabin somewhere in the wilderness. All that I really knew about the state came from a schoolteacher aunt who had driven the Alaska Highway to visit there years earlier. I had learned more from a classmate at a company school who told tales of flying to remote places in very small airplanes. My inquiry about the openings brought a gruff response from the regional manager about his region not training me for some other region to use. If I sought more information, a pending trip to another company school would be cancelled. My local manager suggested that I attend the school and then inquire further.

My then wife was also not in favor of becoming an Alaska resident. Any place with snow and ice that far from California was definitely not on her wish list. Case closed.

After attending the school, I became involved in raising a family, attending law school, and making moves that kept my thoughts close to California. Some sixteen years later when my sister got to Alaska after wearing other places out, I heard a bit more about the state. This rekindled the old dream about living on what was touted as "The Last Frontier." Soon afterwards as my law practice and the marriage closed out, I was in a time and mood to seek new beginnings.

As I packed, a job was offered to me only one hundred miles north of where I was living. Money to feed me and the children I was now raising seemed better than arriving in Alaska with no job. I again delayed heading north. When the interim job ended after a decline in bankruptcies and foreclosures to work on, I finally moved the rest of the way north. A job waiting in Juneau ruled out moving to Fairbanks and a house that I had invested in there. That is how I came to live in the most desirable part of the most desirable state.

This, then, is not the usual book about the Alaska Experience. No bears are ever encountered up too close and personal nor has life in the real bush been faced or even sought. It is, rather, a reflection of adjusting to a place of great natural beauty, extremes of climate, and to the people who deal with both. It is a coming into a lifestyle that merges the pasts of

California and elsewhere with Alaska, its' legends, and its' future.

THE ROAD NORTH
AUGUST, 1984

My contemplated timetable was to leave on August 13, 1984 from Upland, California, for either Fairbanks or Juneau, Alaska. The deciding factor would be whether a state job I had applied for in Juneau was offered to me. If not, on to Fairbanks and hope to find work. Having only travel money plus enough to live on for a few weeks, the firm job was the best option. As of Wednesday, "no firm offer could be made" but "I was the preferred choice." On Thursday, after a sweaty day of moving things into a storage locker, I took the logical step to get a phone call: take a shower. I was told that the job was being offered to me. That led to more frantic preparations in order to report for work a week from the following Monday. As no paved road goes on dry land clear to Juneau, a reservation on the Alaska Marine Highway System had to be made on short notice. During the busy summer season these are normally made at least forty-five days in advance. Or I faced the possibility of leaving the car at the dock for later shipment.

By Saturday the space was confirmed. The same day a trip was made to San Diego so that my kids could visit their seriously ill grandmother, see their mother for her birthday, and so that the cat could be left with the non-custodial parent until I was settled in Juneau. I also attended a monthly men's group service at All Souls in Point Loma, followed by breakfast to say my farewells to old friends of long standing. The kids took their mother to lunch at Dad's expense, visited their grandmother, and shopped. Then we headed back to Upland for Sunday at St. Mark's Church and farewells there. The rest of Sunday was used to get last minute items for the kids and for them to pack John's 1966 Ford pickup. The pickup was to hopefully take Kate, age 16, to school in Montana and John, age 18, to St. Paul Bible College in Minnesota. Going along was Barbie Halverson of Glasgow, Montana, who was to help drive and keep the peace between brother and sister. She had been in California visiting and knew John from several summers at Pines Youth Camp where he had been a camper.

Early Monday morning the last items were loaded into the pickup. John helped with the loading of my king-sized bed onto the top of the station wagon and covering it with a blue plastic cover. With high hopes they left at mid-day for Beaver, Utah. Except for a loose clutch-adjusting bolt near Barstow, California, which John fixed after reading his Chilton manual, they had no problems and were only about eighty miles short of their day's goal when they stopped to camp for the night. In the meantime, now realizing that I was on my own after eighteen years of parenting, I somehow loaded the six foot sofa/hide-a-bed into the station wagon and hoped for a Wednesday departure. I was to be at the dock in Seattle by 3 p.m. Friday. As the Ford wagon was a well-aged fourteen years old with a tendency to run hot, it seemed wise not to push the schedule, i.e. leave some time for repairs. As Monday went, it became obvious that Wednesday would certainly be the earliest that I could leave. Even that estimate proved inaccurate as I wound up packing office items, hauling stuff to the storage place, giving stuff away, consigning items, and wondering when it would all be finished. One striking memory of that time happened as I crammed the final items into the storage unit. A crystal snack dish fell from a Lazy-Susan that I was trying to shove into the top of the loaded locker. It struck my forehead as it fell and probably broke. With that I forced the door shut and locked it. As I drove toward the entrance of the area wondering what to do with the things I wasn't able to store, a lady drove by and asked about the facility. I pointed out where the office was and then asked her if she could use some five gallon plastic water bottles. She said yes and also accepted my work bench stool. Then I inquired if she had any use for a set of golf clubs. Her reply was that her son didn't golf but he sure would now.

With that I headed for the bank to close out things there. At the counter, I noticed that the teller was eyeing me in a questioning way. I realized that I was sweaty, most likely smelled, was unshaved, and wore worn shorts and a T-shirt that were in need of washing and mending. It wasn't till I got to the apartment and faced a mirror that I realized that the falling dish had dented my forehead, which had blood mixed with the sweat. No wonder the teller had eyed me with a wondering look.

On Wednesday night, the apartment was not cleaned, the car was loaded inside and out, and it was too late to go that day. Sleep seemed in order after the efforts of the prior week and in anticipation of a long drive to Seattle. The calls to disconnect the telephone and the utilities had not been made yet. A note was left for the landlord about paying for cleaning the place with the rent deposit; time and energy did not remain in sufficient quantity to do otherwise. Finally, at 4:45 a.m. on Thursday, August 16, 1984, the show got on the road.

For those who have never driven an overloaded Ford wagon with a king-sized bed on the roof rack topped by a tied-down hand truck and fifty feet of garden hose, a six-foot sofa in the back and every place inside crammed with dishes, clothes, many other housewares, and fishing tackle (like a moving garage sale), just imagine the world's largest skateboard with mirrors. The passenger side mirror was a remnant of boat trailer pulling and was tied on with bungee cords. I could view it through a lamp shade on the seat next to me. I had neglected to put on air shocks or bags which might have kept the rear bumper from being close to ground zero so the hood slanted up several degrees. When I entered the freeway, I noticed that any speed over fifty miles an hour revealed basic problems in directional stability which called for constant corrections. I began to wonder if undertaking the drive was a sound decision.

By the time that the sun was starting to fight the smog over the Los Angeles basin, I was on the way up the Grapevine trying nervously to steer and also watch an extra temperature gauge I had installed in the only available spot. I had to twist my neck and look down to see it. To my amazement the engine temperature never climbed past the normal range as I drove up the long upgrades before downshifting to keep my speed under fifty miles an hour to avoid losing control down the other side. The only problem occurred as I came down the Grapevine and started towards Bakersfield. A passing driver honked and pointed at the back of the wagon. I found a place to pull over and see what had happened. I found that one end of the garden hose had escaped and was now trailing fifty feet behind me. At least the hand truck was still on top of the load.

The rest of the morning and the early afternoon was spent driving north through the San Joaquin Valley. Somewhere there was a breakfast stop with a scrape in and out of the parking lot, a gas stop, and a stop to check a belt squeak. As it only made noise while in the slow lane, I resolved to press on in the fast lane and not worry. Sacramento was sighted somewhere in early afternoon, and as things were progressing with the help of occasional stops for coffee or tea and disposal thereof, moving on seemed in order.

By 2:30 p.m. I was at a rest stop in Williams and feeling like going on and perhaps getting to Redding or even Mt. Shasta before dark. Maybe it would even be possible to get out of the state while I was still lucid. Even a food and gas stop in Willows did not discourage me. This was my territory in the good old days of General Adjustment Bureau, Chico, where the kids had first arrived on the scene. The fresh air and the harvest smells, after Southern California smog, seemed like the start of a new era. The Castle Crags near Dunsmuir and Mt Shasta, lit by the setting sun were spectacular in their beauty. Another rest stop, courtesy of Cal Trans, and on to Medford, Oregon, by 9 p.m. I stopped for dinner and more gas and wondered how much longer I could last without being a menace on the road. My time margin of eight spare hours had dwindled to where only five or six extra hours remained. The map showed about three hundred miles of Oregon road over various passes before Washington State became a reality. I managed two more hours of forward movement before finding another Denny's (I think by now I have seen them all) for coffee and a restroom. After that I tried to get off the freeway in a small town to nap but a state trooper came on the scene and gave me the mileage to a real rest stop rather than the foot of the off ramp. When I finally gave up at about 2 a.m., I had to sleep with my feet out the driver's window, as there was no room in the front seat to do otherwise without evicting the TV, lampshades, Dutch oven, bedroll, and a few other items. After two hours sleep, I moved on and was able to find Portland, Oregon and face the early rush hour traffic. Breakfast took away more of the time margin. With only 175 miles to go to Seattle, my thought was that anything adverse mechanically that was to happen would have already happened, so why worry. With only the winds of a few high crossings over water to contend with, the end of the journey seemed in sight. At last the goal loomed ahead, Seattle, Kingdome and all, but the shell of my former being was too tired to contend with the downtown elevated freeway system. I decided to try side streets at lower levels and ended up in the main business district looking for a way to Pier 48. Somehow I cut a corner short enough to contact a curb, heard a hissing of air, and uttered a few descriptive words. The tires were not that great but had been alright for

Seattle if not the Alaska Highway. I wearily climbed out thinking of how I could get the spare out without unloading the sofa. When I looked at the tire it was fine. The noise was coming fitfully from the exhaust pipe which had been crushed closed when it hit the curb. Out with the sombrero, lampshades, Dutch oven, bedroll, and other front seat cargo to get to my toolbox and find exhaust pipe opening tools. I managed to use the pointy end of a lug wrench and a hammer to pry the tailpipe open. All of this happened in a no parking zone while shoppers and cars buzzed around me. After the pipe was open enough for the car to run smoothly, I re-packed the front seat and headed for Pier 48, where I arrived two hours before sailing - except that with their time change, I was really only an hour early.

After checking in and waiting for two hours, the walk-on passengers without cars were allowed to board and thereby get the premium places on the solarium deck for camping. By the time I drove onto the car deck, got bags and sleeping stuff out and found the passenger areas, the solarium at the bow of the ship looked like a KOA advertisement.

I retreated to a corner of the Observation Deck lounge and set up housekeeping in a corner for resting during the fifty-six hour run to Juneau. The MV Columbia sailed at 6 p.m., which gave me an opportunity to see the area at water level. It was sort of like San Diego except with more trees. I was not so tired that I couldn't recognize the Space Needle, which seemed quite close to the water. After the ship cleared the harbor, I practiced sleeping on the floor. It was quite an improvement over the previous night; at least I could stretch out.

Early Saturday found the ship winding a course between fog-shrouded islands, with homes and fishing boats adding to the scene. That scenery kept up most of the day and could be seen through the rain, which arrived as promised. By that time I had found the public shower used by we walk-ons and could stand next to myself again. The day was used to watch the trees on the shore come and go, to find that the food in the snack bar was good if expensive, and to learn that naps during the day were inhibited by legions of small kids whose parents turned them loose and disappeared. Dinner was a reasonable shrimp curry in the main dining room with a price tag of under $10.00 for the meal, which was a pleasant surprise. Sunday morning at 7 a.m. the ship pulled into Ketchikan followed by stops in Wrangall and Petersburg. Finally, at 2:30 a.m. Monday morning, the ship docked in Auke Bay about fourteen miles north of Juneau. I descended to the car deck, drove off the ship, and headed down a dark, rainy, and windy road to my new home city. Everything was closed except for one hotel where I was told the rate was $98.00 for a single, but "I could get a nice place elsewhere for $64.00, the "government rate." I opted to park on a motel lot till the place opened and was approached by an acquaintance from the ship who was coming to Juneau for Coast Guard duty. He was now showing signs of being loaded as he had received news about the death of a brother he had just visited in Florida. He took me in tow and arranged for me to get coffee at the nearby Coast Guard station and to later be able to take a shower there. I could not change to a suit as that was contrary to regulations for a civilian to do. Somehow, as he wandered down a hall, he hit the general quarters alarm button and woke up the chief in charge who charged out in his skivvies. The two turned out to be old buddies. Later my friend's wife showed up looking for him and we managed to find a place for breakfast. Afterwards I borrowed a motel room from another couple off the ship to change into a suit and tie. Then it was off to the new job at 8 a.m., followed by a week of catching up on lost rest.

HOUSING
AUGUST 20, 1984

After spending the last night on the Columbia sleeping in a lounge chair before docking in Auke Bay and drinking coffee at the Coast Guard Station in Juneau, I was not well rested when I reported to my new job. I vaguely recall meeting the people that I would be working with, attending a weekly staff meeting, and being taken to the tenth floor of the State Office Building (called the SOB) for in-processing. Forms and papers that I signed were a blur. The return to the office area was a chance to learn more about who I would be working with. One of the team that had interviewed me in Anchorage a few weeks earlier and had asked if I knew that the job didn't offer much upward mobility had since resigned to take a job "Outside" that offered better potential. The word "outside" caused me to think of the Ford parked on a nearby street in the rain with the mattress on top. Having made no progress toward finding a motel to stay in while I looked for an apartment, I inquired about what might be a good place to stay. Someone mentioned that a co-worker might have a room I could use if her husband agreed. After work I followed them to their home out on Douglas Island in a tract called Bonnie Brae and found that a downstairs room next to a bathroom offered an ideal interim solution. It also gave me a chance to unload the Ford and see what I had brought. After the one-car garage was filled, the host showed added amazement that it had all been in and on the Ford.

After a few nights of rest, the need for long-term housing was given more thought. Ads were read, location and prices studied, and I started making the rounds. The first place I looked was in the community of Douglas across the channel from downtown Juneau. It had one bathroom with three basins, two toilets, and a shower stall eight feet long with a shower head at each end. It had been set up for a gaggle of daughters that had moved on. Parking was an issue. A place out in the Mendenhall Valley had a cramped floor plan. One out on North Douglas looked nice from the road but the rent was over the market and my budget. The inside made that of less concern as it was the right size, was close to town but not in it, had a view, and very important, was available at once. Richard and Mindy Lee, owners of the Silverbow Inn downtown, would be my landlords.

So the stuff in the garage at the Carson's was emptied back into the wagon and the move was made as Labor Day weekend rolled around. With the much appreciated help of a friend from Fairbanks who came down with her children, I got the stuff in and started unpacking. The first dinner was hampered by not being able to find a knife or a can opener. Those things had to be borrowed along with chairs and blankets. Saturday and Sunday were used to tour Juneau and do more unpacking.

The choice for church affiliation in my new home town was essentially one. The local Episcopal church was in the downtown area but it also offered Sunday services in the valley area at a high school. No one had apparently raised the church and state issue. As the valley had become the population center, many of the parishioners attend "out the road." The downtown group met at the downtown church at Fourth and Gold in an edifice of history and beauty built in 1896 as the second church building in Juneau. I met the interim rector one day when I returned to my cubicle at work and found him waiting for me. The color of his somewhat faded maroon vest indicated that he was a bishop, active or retired. He had apparently been invited to my cubicle by my boss who was also the senior warden at Holy Trinity. Having never before had the experience of meeting a retired bishop in my cubicle, I attended the service on the next Sunday. Soon I was taking my Polish Sausage and Cabbage recipe to potlucks at the church, singing in the choir (God even loves a monotone) and serving as a reader and chalice bearer, even before I had completed my year at St. Marks in Upland. In less than a quarter year in Juneau, I found myself in the midst of an active parish with dedicated members trying to do their mission with limited resources.

THE GREAT LAND - SOUTHEAST
OCTOBER 14, 1984

Two months, nearly, in the North, The Great Land. Not "The Bush" because that is further away even if never too far away in thought or actuality. To Alaskans it is a state of mind if not an actuality that conjures up thoughts of small isolated villages or cabins where people live under the most rugged conditions. Even in the "major" population centers, one can be out of town a few miles by air or boat and in the bush in an hour or less. Time to return might be something else. But the real Bush is a world apart from the relative comfort of a city like Juneau which doesn't really lack in things people Outside have. Except possibly fishing reel parts and the latest power tools.

No snow yet and no really cold days. Ice on the windshield only once so far. Cool in the a.m., more so when fishing, or at least on the hands. But winter is a-coming. Not like the icy realm of Fairbanks a thousand miles further North and certainly not like Barrow on the North Slope another nine hundred miles north where it never warms up to where we are now. But on the way. Yesterday was the day I bought my Sorrels. Do Southern Californians know about Sorrels and other related waffle stompers that are a way of life here? It was also time to put snow tires on the back of the wagon and start getting used to the hum. I'm glad to learn that the state troopers use the same brand of tire. Do they endure the hum year round in some places? So far the tab for rain gear and snow gear (at 40% off on everything) nears $200. For one person. How do the folks with families do it? Even with the "average" household income here exceeding $50,000, it must be a challenge. A largely affluent society next to a glacier.

Where the difference in life here and there ("there" having been Southern California with time off for good behavior in Sacramento part of that twenty years) is that you can encounter a lot of the same potential dangers to life and limb there but here they are a lot closer. More constant and more immediately hazardous. Such as my nearby fishing grounds out on the tidal flats at Salmon Creek off Egan Drive. Just to get from the parking place near the TV tower and station at 3 and ½ mile where the mud is classic and deep, to the tidal flats, one picks a cautious descent down a steep rubble-strewn embankment. When climbing back up later with fishing gear, and perhaps fish, in rain and darkness and cold tiredness, the thought comes that a slip could easily wipe out a knee or some other part. Yesterday, at first light, going upstream (not to spawn), the rocks under the Egan Drive Bridge were moss-slick. The water is only a foot or two deep, but the speed of the current as low tide comes on is swift beyond most of my stream walking experience. A lot faster than the crick on the farm is Southwest Missouri of boyhood summers. Slow steps and plant feet firmly or accept disaster. How much water can waders hold? Later, when out on the flats and casting into deeper water, I realize that the water is icy cold year round. If not glacier fed, it is mountain snow runoff and boots or waders can fill. Incipient hypothermia, winter or summer, is a fact in this land. The knife on the belt which hasn't been used very often to clean fish with is also a handy item in case of a fall where the boots or waders need to be cut off. A wool hat or the hood on the sweatshirt under the rain gear protects against loss of body heat by the scalp route. It is probably not too wise to stay in the channel water after or before other fisher people are present. Someone should at least see you floating off. My final lesson came one morning when I tarried long enough in the water for the incoming tide to fill my boots. I managed to get back to the wagon and lower the tailgate to sit on. As I raised my legs to pull the boots off, the icy water was channeled down inside my jeans causing me to stand up immediately and drain the water out. I drove home in record time and changed clothes very quickly.

Now I even think of arming myself - not because of people, but because of the fact that any excursion off the road for fishing, berry picking or hiking can introduce one to the resident bear, which, after all, was here first. Bears, in my pre-Alaska days, were big things that lived in Yellowstone National Park and something not to be fed when touring there. Here they are not to be fed anytime. By and large these same dangers or their local equivalents exist elsewhere but you may have to go further to find them. There, the advice may be to not leave home without your credit card; here, not without your rain gear and other survival items. The mere thought of owning a gun is an acknowledgment of such a life style. Except for the ones loaned to me by the army during my six years of service time, including at one time a .38 caliber detective special with no safety except the holster strap, I have not owned a gun since the .22 caliber single shot rifle of my rabbit hunting and Boy Scout days. Now I think of shopping for a .357 that Magnum PI would be proud of. So far, however, I have no 4 X 4 pickup with the gun rack which state law or custom seems to require within six months of arrival.

More important than that, perhaps, is each person's personal hat collection. So far I have added to what I had when I got off the boat: a baseball hat (UA-Juneau) which was last seen after it blew off while fishing, a wool watch cap, a rain hat for formal occasions, such as going to church or work, my parka hood, and a Sou'wester which covers everything except incipient hair loss. Again, you don't leave the house without one or two. The bareheaded days are by and large gone, a part of Southern California memories. If your blue jean/Levi wardrobe formerly consisted of one good pair plus a faded pair for backup use, you are in trouble. The minimum here is one pair on, one pair drying, one pair muddy, and a spare to fill in one of the slots. Welcome to the land of wood stoves, even with electric heat in the house, tide charts, and an ear to the weather reports.

Motor vehicle operational management, aka driving, is also a constant reminder of the Alaska scene. Snow, ice, and rain and the skills needed to stay on the road are a part of my Midwest heritage. Here, however, the conditions are ongoing. Rain almost daily during much of the non-snow season (a dry spell is four hours without rain) and snow the rest of the year makes for wet windows outside and steamy ones inside the car. The effect is enhanced by long dark nights, which, with the wet or snowy or icy pavements, gives statistical assurance of some ultimate crunching of the car exterior. To paraphrase the country and western hit, "If drinking don't get you, the memories will", here it's "If the rust don't get you, the other driver will." It is all just part of life on the comfortable Last Frontier.

THE WOOD LOT: COMMUNITY IN ACTION
OCTOBER 20, 1984

My introduction to volunteerism in my new state came when I responded to a need for volunteers to help in the annual firewood sale of a local group raising funds for abused and battered women's programs. The only problem was finding the landfill/city dump out at Lemon Creek between town and valley. (The turnoff is not marked as "everyone knows where it is, just look for the seagulls.") Following several large trash trucks finally led me to the place. After checking in, I was assigned a chainsaw that needed work. Having no prior chainsaw experience other than knowing what one looks like, it seemed like it might be a learning experience. As it was on loan to the project, there were no instructions about starting it, using it, or what the proper fuel/oil ratio might be. The wrong choice could cause either a fouled sparkplug or a burned-out engine. While I was trying to decide which coin to toss, I was redirected to a log splitter. The rental units were just arriving. Another gas-powered device that I had not used before. After noting that Honda was even in that field, I joined two women as the team on a machine. Even with their Juneau tennies, faded jeans, bulky sweat shirts, and no makeup it was possible to tell the difference. What amazed me, being used to the belles of Southern California, was that the lifting of the log rounds up to the splitter was undertaken by one of the women. None of the "you do the heavy stuff, we will bring the coffee and donuts" outlook. And they did just as good a job as the men, perhaps better. Another bit of welcome to Alaska. We proceeded into the morning amid the roar of the saws, the crunch of the splitter, and dropping of pieces onto our pile. I made an effort to stack neatly, but was admonished that neat does not count, a cord is measured by eyeball. Close to noon I was asked to go along on a delivery out on North Douglas. The Toyota pickup was driven by John, a jailhouse counselor with two MS degrees and a mid-section in which gravity was working overtime. He was happy to have a talker along as the prior helper did not. I learned that he also fishes and will even snag a few if his freezer is low. He came to Alaska because of better pay here but has turned into a booster of the state. His words were also colorful. Sour Donkey what? We dumped the wood down an embankment near a roadside pulloff and then went to find "Walter's old cabin" where the wood buyer lived. First, we went down a raised wooden runway toward the channel for a quarter mile. The runway had no rail as it meandered over the lowland and through the trees. Why not a raised sort of sidewalk to keep out the flora and fauna? Before coming to a main house, we turned off of the wide walk onto one made of two by twelves that angled at various degrees toward an ancient cabin. Not a place to walk at night without light and with spirits aboard. No water in the cabin but it does have electricity. The wood is for heating and will be carried back in a garden wheelbarrow. Mother and child and no indoor plumbing, but no complaints about how tough things are.

After taking a second load to the same place, a break was taken to eat donated pizza from Bullwinkle's and to drink donated orange drink from McDonalds. First pineapple pizza I have ever had but why not? Back to the splitter where I was able to do some of the lifting without being pushy. About 4 p.m. I wondered if this was what I wanted to spend the rest of my life doing - would it ever be sundown? Salvation arrived in the form of being asked if I could go along on the delivery of four cords. The large truck was owned and driven by Mike, a University of Alaska student whose wife works for the state. The fact that he sort of runs a bootleg trucking service and has a lack of insurance and needs a new front tire to replace the bumpy one came after we got to freeway speed on Egan Drive. He spent about eight years in the Coast Guard, part of that time in Alaska, and came back here after his mustering out. I was pleased to learn that he talks to his truck the way that I talk to my station wagon: when your vehicle has shared a cross-country move with you, it begins to take on a personality of its' own. We dumped three cords at a place where the buyer offered a choice of coffee or beer and moved on to the last stop of the day. This stop was in the middle of a valley suburb that could match any such place in San Jose or Orange County. The man of the house had the usual state parking sticker on his VW Rabbit and sort of seemed to be the non-adventurer type who is here for the job. (Maybe he is really a native of the state.) His wife appeared amply fed. Their small child enjoyed being in the danger zone near the truck where wood was falling and failed to heed motherly calls to be careful. With good fortune, we managed not to drop any logs on him as the work went on. After getting back to the dump and finding the gate closed, we sort of went in the wrong way so that we could turn in the money and check out. All in all a good day. No sore muscles, new friends and a feeling that barn raising type things are alive and well here.

PRELUDE TO WINTER
OCTOBER 28 - 30, 1984

Now we are in that period between still fall but not officially winter, where, like an orchestra tuning up, there are little bits of all that will be heard later in unison. The rains have ceased as much as they ever do in the realm of Juneau. High winds last week scoured the town and mountains. As the winds faded, cold air swept in and has not moved on. Snow sits on the higher slopes waiting its' turn. During this hiatus, the sun bathes all in crisp clarity.

Off to church on Sunday and a 22 degree reading outside my door. The car starts readily; it is a day to day guess as to when the aged battery will give out. Block heaters don't seem as common here as in Anchorage and Fairbanks. The day is brisk, clear, and ice-breezed. A Monday drive to the post office at Auke Bay and passing 4 ½ mile Egan Drive is a panorama of snow-crested mountains to the northwest past the end of Douglas Island toward Admiralty Island, if my directions are right. The snowline creeps lower nightly. Time to tie down the trash cans or loose them. And to perhaps warm up the car while having morning coffee. The orange posts with reflector tape to guide the snow removers are now planted along Egan Drive. At least the posts don't seem to be as tall as those in other parts of the state.

The onset of winter does not alarm one who has wintered in Kansas, Wyoming, and West Germany. But it is a far cry from the Southern California beaches of the last twenty years. Here it is ice in the mop bucket if left outside and ice along the beaches at low tide. There is new appreciation for learning about winter in the North by a short time spent in Fairbanks before coming to Juneau.

Tuesday morning and the trek up to the living level of the house, as opposed to the lower sleeping level. The voice on the radio announces that the 13 degrees overnight is a record for the date. Alaskans take pride in their ability to accept such news without slowing down. It is warm inside anyway. Head for the shower and realize that no water is coming out, which seems to be a clear indication that it is not as warm outside around pipes, pump, or tank. Where does that leave the car? It was fine at 22 degrees, but the new low record is below that. And the lack of water could affect shaving. Time to consider alternatives. If there was a place to do the morning necessaries, which might be as necessary as usual, would I be able to get someplace to do them? Back to the sleeping level, dress for the occasion, not the office. Trudge out to the wagon to see how it is fairing. No hesitation there; it starts like cold weather is no problem at all. Now I can go to work or elsewhere, even if not properly brushed and combed. Inspiration dawns. Call friends and ask to borrow a cup of shower. Sure; in Alaska such calls are the norm. Out to bathe and then back home to dress for work and to have the part of breakfast that does not need water. There's coffee at the office anyway. Warmth of home and office so close to the realities of the environment outside with more realities to come. Part of the continuing education of the Cheechako. The knowledge that wanting to live in this great land requires an acceptance of its' nature. And that it is well worth the cost.

RESTAURANTS
NOVEMBER 2, 1984

Whether a person moves to Alaska, or only a few hours driving time from where he or she moved from in our mobile society, dining out under the new circumstances can be one of the more adventuresome parts of scouting the new territory. That is, once you realize that McDonald's and Denny's and Orange Julius never vary, you are on your own. And perhaps at the mercy of those places that, like some people, look interesting initially but don't meet what the words on the menu propounded.

My pre-Alaska training in this field was received mainly in Sacramento, San Diego, San Francisco, and Upland, California (where is Upland?) with some very limited basic training in Kansas. Until I entered the army, I thought that all shrimp were caught breaded and that beef was born burned. I had never had any pasta. When I settled for a time in California, a few places of consistently good food and quality service were found, to which I could return if and when in the area, with the exception of those in Chico and Yuba City ,which were not restaurant type eateries. Places such as Original Mac's in Sacramento for lunch, The Shadows in San

Francisco - if the place still exists, the Cotton Patch in San Diego for steak with all the fore and aft parts of a great meal, the Fish Factory in Del Mar for prawns in garlic butter and with sour dough bread, Kowloon in Upland for Kung Pao chicken. Now, however, it is time to find out what Alaska offers, aside from the regional home-cooked specialties of Bambi and bear and Halibut.

As a start I had dinner at Ivory Jack's in Fairbanks on a minus 23 degree night last February. Having had an interesting and charming lady along, I don't remember much about the place except that the fare was good - bad food I would have remembered regardless of the company. I do remember the unique front door handle, which is something that makes a first date quite interesting conversation-wise. Some male walrus was now coming up short. The occasion was the first time in years (or the only time?) where a diner at an adjacent table was passed out face down in his plate. His four companions carried on eating and drinking until done with their meals. Then they pried his face out of his plate and carried him out. During the trip, I had also dined at the Westward Hilton in Anchorage and, aside from toxic price shock syndrome, found the food to be equal to or better than many places Outside. I also enjoyed the Downtown Deli and Café there for breakfast; there are not many non-hotel breakfast spots in the downtown area.

The Juneau tour so far has been hit and miss. A Mexican dinner at Casa del Sol was Tex-Mex-Tourist fare, but not much more taste-wise than similar places in other states including California. A bit of Carlos Murphy's in the North. For refried beans though, those at Olivia's de Mexico in the lower level of the Simpson Building in downtown Juneau were a welcome find. And somewhere along the line, in spite of its' advertising, I found that Yancy Derringer's has good clam chowder and beer-battered seafood that is first rate. The best hamburgers are those served at the University of Alaska Southeast cafeteria and were worth a noon trip out to Auke Bay. My research was set back a notch by a visit to Oriental Gardens out in the Valley, that being where the commuters live. After getting my warmies back on when it appeared that no waitress would ever trip over my table, I was rash enough to stay and to ask to see a menu, not knowing what was offered. Almond chicken seemed safe. What could be done to it? I soon learned. First came the only Chinese soup I have ever had with a thin layer of grease on the surface. If it was egg flower soup, the egg was wilted. The salt in it would have floated a won ton. Halfway through it, I surrendered. The main course arrived with rice of a yellow hue for some reason. This was not a place that was likely to use saffron. The almond chicken was bathed in a brown gravy of the type used to cover hot roast beef sandwiches in Kansas in the fifties. Chinese it was not. But at least it covered the chicken which was breaded and deep fried. The almond ambience was provided by chopped almonds sprinkled on top of the gravy. In my distress I accepted the offering, then had to find the waitress to get hot tea. Which turned out to be a lonely Lipton tea bag lost in a large teapot while trying to turn into tea. The tea was poured into a coffee mug rather than a tea cup, Chinese or otherwise. I will never know if I caught the place on a bad night, as there are too many places in Juneau where the food is not of such unique character. The wrinkled high-mileage menu should have been the first clue.

Where it leaves a new-to-Juneau diner is with a realization that overall the food and places are equal to any other city here or Outside. That works both ways as to quality and service. There is more of a tendency here to put a restaurant in an out-of-the-way place such as a basement or on the upper level of a remote office building. Casa del Sol is over the State Trooper Detachment, which is convenient for sobriety tests before the drive home gets underway. At least it is a good reminder. My one bad dining experience so far will not keep me from my appointed rounds of finding the local spots where, if I ever leave this bit of the best part of Alaska, there will be places to come back to - or to write about from afar.

DIGGING IN BEFORE DIGGING OUT
NOVEMBER 4, 1984

Sunday brought the first snow of the season to our town, at least the first that was low enough down the mountains to be on us, not just as a scenic topping to the green slopes above us, which are now streaked with the ice of frozen streams. A few flakes were spun against the car on the way into Juneau proper for church. During the service, enough fell to cover car and windows and to make descending Main Street down toward the channel a time for caution in driving or walking. Of course the whole spectacular white scene is washed away by rains that come on overnight. But it tells of the time to come when damp streets may in reality be black ice. So slower is in order. With this final acknowledgment of the season, after nearly three months here, I dig in more firmly, not just for the challenge of the expected Taku winds of November, but as a resident of Juneau and as an Alaskan. Now a walk downtown more often than not results in seeing and greeting someone known by sight or in person. The people lodged in the State Office Building during the day are seen around town or in the Valley in different roles after hours.

Breakfast at the Prospector one morning - and by now the words overheard between cashier and customer are recognized as part of the local dialect - Le Conte, Aurora (ships of the Alaska Marine Highway System), run south, shipment coming up on the barge. Restaurants are visited for a second or third time and become known. When a person mentions where they work, you have heard of it and maybe even have been there. I have also learned the slow times at the Laundromat when machines are more available, determined not to grocery shop on Sunday because by then the freshest veggies are gone and the 'MORE MILK MONDAY' sign announces a sold-out item. Soft broccoli and tired tomatoes are incentive to stocking up or Friday buying. I am also learning that grocery buying downtown is a social experience where more time is spent talking than in the actual shopping.

A routine has evolved of work, classes, taking part in being a Juneauite, no longer being the newest kid on the block. Time enough to have made a few friendships with people at work, in class, at church, and in the Singles Again Support Group. Such as an invitation from a classmate employed by the Forest Service to take part in an informal pig roast his co-workers are having at Skater's Cabin on Saturday. Coffee with friends from the singles group at a member's home after a meeting. A nice evening and an invitation to help dress deer that another new friend has brought back from hunting and which offers a chance to learn how it is done. In case I ever bring one back in a stage that requires dressing. Perhaps my success rate in fishing requires a change of venue to venison. On the entertainment scene, going to a play at Juneau-Douglas High School I am amazed at the quality of the performance - and run into my landlord who is two rows ahead of me.

New experiences continue, such as learning about frozen car door locks - the reason even non-smokers carry lighters - and realizing how much glass a full size station wagon has to scrape ice from several times a day. The black ice that results from rain and freezing is cause to realize that snow to drive on is preferable. I also learn that, far away from the smog of the Los Angeles Basin, the people in the Valley are on notice not to burn their firewood this weekend because of potential air pollution due to something called an inversion layer. We on Douglas Island are not so restricted.

So, with work, church, friends, and projects, life takes on a pattern of normalcy that hasn't been part of it for a while, even since San Diego. Because this is a place to stay, not limited by the job uncertainty of Upland or the leaving of San Diego after an end to a marriage and a business venture and an era. On to becoming an Alaskan in interests as well as intent. The best is yet to come.

ON QUARTERING DEER
NOVEMBER 11, 1984

We Alaskans drink a lot of coffee, an awful lot, in fact. This consumption rate comes home to me at 5 a.m. Sunday when, after a day of cutting, cleaning, and de-fatting of dead deer, followed by an evening out, followed by more coffee, I come wide awake at that time. Perhaps the coffee is to blame, perhaps it is thinking of my first encounter with how hunters get the bounty from the field of battle to the dining table. And how coffee is involved in the process.

Coffee, in my Southern California and elsewhere life, was a take it or leave it thing. A cup before leaving for the office and some during the day but seldom finishing a cup before it was cold. Here the pot is always on wherever you are, be it at a meeting, at the office, or with friends. Such as when I drove out to the Valley Saturday to hopefully be of help in reducing seven deer to package-size form. Before leaving, though, during and after a Saturday breakfast of hot cakes, eggs, and bacon as a treat for enduring the weekday diet of cold cereal, juice, and English muffin, two cups of coffee were enjoyed.

Then on out to the Valley, after time spent scraping ice from the wagon windows and thawing the door locks and openers. The place where the deer were hanging in their skinless state was in a garage at the home of a lady who had just completed her divorce and is working and attending college while raising her children. She is a friend from the Singles Again Support Group, as is her friend who organized the deer party so that the project could be completed before spring. He is a member of the same group and had his son, age 12, with him for the weekend. The son is the oldest child present and is a young Alaskan who hunts with his dad and can clean deer along with the rest of us. The couple are friends who are at that post-divorce stage where each is working out the problems brought into their lives by their respective divorces and are not yet at a time when new commitments are in order - yet at a time when friendship and sharing is a way of support and coping until further decisions can be made. The friendship will remain regardless of where the relationship goes. Her three kids are watching Saturday cartoons just like kids in the lower 48, next to a computer keyboard in the living room.

So we coffee up in the kitchen, or mug up as Gordon Nelson, author of "Low Bush Moose" would describe it, for a while until the third older deer cutter arrives with wife and kids and adds two more children to the family room crowd. The new arrival reminds me of my cousin Oren, who long ago taught me whatever I know about hunting. There is no doubt that this person goes out to hunt in a knowing way and does not return empty-handed, unlike the once-a-year urban cowboy who hunts for a place to drink and brag. We drink more coffee, talk about where the deer came from, how some were skinned before leaving the island and some on the boat on the way back. Plans are made to do some clamming, tonight or the next, and after four cups or so of coffee, off to the garage to start the work. Four skinned deer are strung by the front legs from the rafters; three more are in another garage.

Each deer was very quickly divided into quarters as the rear legs were cut from each carcass using a sharp knife, a meat saw, and skill at locating the joints. Then a rack of ribs was cut from each side of the backbone before removing the forelegs. This left the backstrap with the remaining rib portions on either side. My task was to take the parts to the kitchen for the next step, which was preceded by more coffee.

The goal was to come up with venison steaks, chops, roasts, ribs, stew meat, meat for grinding into deerburger meat, and bones for boiling the marrow out of for stock. The many scraps are not kept for the dogs, as rich meat can cause problems if the animal is allowed to stay indoors after eating it. It is too cold to keep the door open to let fresh air in to solve the problem. The kitchen becomes a collage of sharp knives, moving knife sharpeners, boxes for fat and for bones, piles of meat not yet carved and piles of meat that are chops and roasts and steaks. The card table sags a bit under the weight of the stuff piled on it and the kids are running through like Indians around the wagons. Much of the work involves removing the fat because it becomes rancid earlier than fat on beef. The layers of fat bring comments that it looks like a long, cold winter. So we cut, saw, trim fat, and drink coffee. The coffee mug is never empty or cold. Sometime during the afternoon there is a break for a lunch of fresh venison steak and cottage fried potatoes. The younger kids, after the mandatory fights and boredom, are quiet with the computer games, a nice counterpoint to the ancient process going on in the kitchen. By 5:30 the work on the first four deer is at a point where the wrappers take over and I, after coffee, go out to defrost the car again.

Then back to town, accompanied by a bag of ribs, chops, and steaks, and off to a play with a friend. And coffee with conversation afterwards before returning home, but not to more coffee; that will have to wait until full morning when the cycle starts again. And then, after church, coffee hour...

BOOTS
NOVEMBER 12, 1984

The song may have stated "These boots are made for walking..." but that is not the whole truth in our state. Until I arrived on the Last Frontier, my experience with boots had been largely confined to those tall leather combat boots with large soles issued to me during my time in the military. As I recall, they were issued in brown and had to be dyed black before spit polishing and wearing them. Which makes about as much sense as anything else I can remember about that six-year period. One pair is still with me, still black, and, as it has been twenty-four years since the last mustering out, they do last. Of course, unless the job calls for it or one is spending time marching as a civilian, boots don't get a lot of miles on them in the lower forty-eight.

In any event, shortly after arriving in Juneau, I found that city shoes and so-called desert boots are not the first choice for walking across the tidal flats at Salmon Creek to pursue fish that other people are catching. Not only do they sink below their tops in the tidal muck, but it is almost impossible to get the muck smell out of them. Even when ostensibly clean, when worn at

McDonald's, people turn around and look at them. As a result, I quickly invested in Juneau Tennies, which are the knee-high rubber boots worn on boat decks and in barnyards. They are part of the local scenery everywhere here, including church. Pants are tucked into them or worn outside of them if the rain is not too heavy. I was now able to get out in the water to cast further and able to not worry about crossing the flats or wading through the mud of the parking area. However, on one occasion, a few missed rocks and high tide caused the water level to exceed the total height of the new boots, so water thereby entered to the previously dry sock area. When I sat on the wagon tailgate to empty them, I chilled various areas of my lower half as the water drained into my jeans. What followed was the quickest drive so far from the fishing area to home to change and warm up.

To solve such problems, the next step was into hip boots, which keep water out at deeper levels. Except that they hold more when full, so a fishing knife is kept on my belt in case of falling into the murky channel waters. The boots are also great for stuffing hats and gloves down into while fishing. They are the answer to getting out to where the big fish swim by you on their way to being caught by people on the shore.

The arrival of winter also caused me to invest in a pair of Sorels, which are the rubber-bottomed, leather upper, felt-lined boots for an arctic winter. They are as common in offices, church or elsewhere as the Juneau Tennies and somewhat more dressy. Today was the trial run for my pair as we get into the snow season. I know now what all boots have in common. They require more than a full-size car when you drive anywhere. Entering and leaving the wagon requires careful sitting and maneuvering to even gain entry or exit. With the thick soles and felt liners, the car pedals are an inch further away from sensitivity. Like an older person who has less feeling in the feet, it is at first an all or nothing feeling on the gas and brake pedals. While it makes for an interesting ride on ice, it can be a problem. One tends to feel like the toy doll that can't be knocked over; there is so much down there for support. And, while coping with large boots on small pedals, there is also dealing with slowly defrosting windows which may be clear by the time you get to work and doors that thaw out and open suddenly as you turn a corner. With time I will become accustomed to lacing up in the morning, pivoting into the car, and being sure I have used elastic cords to secure the doors. It's part of the fun of being in a new place to adapt to such parts of the local and state scene. Now, if I can learn the difference between bunny boots and moon boots, I will be ready for the winter.

A RAINY NIGHT IN JUNEAU NOVEMBER 20, 1984

Two more shopping days until Thanksgiving and, with the exception of the brief Sunday snow two weeks ago, winter in the Frozen North has not produced any problems for me or the Ford. Yet. There are still five months or more for me to see what I have missed so far. As Uncle Fats says on the radio early in the a.m., "Count every day you don't have to shovel snow or scrape your windshield as a blessing." Last night was just a bit windy; wonder why the airlines had to fly by without landing? I learned of this when the dentist's office called at 7 a.m. to reschedule me as the doctor's wife was on a flight that didn't land. He had to do the child shuttling in her place. Yesterday was an eye exam; with the health coverage that was not a part of the years of lawyering, there is a tendency to try to catch up on what has been missed. Like a cowpoke hitting town on a Saturday night after a week out on the range. The eye doctor has fished out of two places in Baja California that I have also been to. Small world department. He inquired as to whether I have my own plane; my suit vest must have been his clue. The boating magazine in his reception room advertises non-skid wineglasses. Won't spill up to twenty degrees, won't slide until 25 degrees. At that point I would put the cap back on the bottle or the cork back in or finish the bottle. Something for everyone in the society.

Tonight has been a saga of frustration as I drove out to the Valley to run errands. What you buy at Fred Meyer on Saturday can be exchanged for what you wanted on Tuesday. If the State credited time spent in Fred Meyer toward retirement, we state employees would all retire a year or two sooner. The three-way light bulb that doesn't has to be taken back to the hardware customer service; they like to do their own returns. The T-shirts which I bought on sale to be the first layer of insulation after fat and skin, after twenty years of not messing with them, are the wrong size because they were in the wrong bin and who checks the label on the package. They must be exchanged at the main customer service area. Except that they don't have the right size anyway, nor do they have the Levi 501s ordered for my daughter. Or the pie sizing plastic sheet or the cookbook or the crust pincher tool. Then there is a lengthy wait while the lay-a-ways ahead of me are processed. And they need an ID from me. Which makes me aware that here on the Last Frontier I am more ID'd than ever in California. Do you accept the Alaska Driver's license, or do you prefer the state employee's ID card - it has a better photo - or the University of

Alaska student card? Sorry, no photo on the voter's registration card used to claim a ballot with. Then the paperwork is done but has to be redone as the returned items were bought at sale price and I pointed this out before starting the process. Then to the cashier to apply the voucher toward the purchase of items I most likely would not have bought except for the extra trip to the store. And I find that the sale price on a novelty T-shirt hasn't hit the computer. So a call to the department. Are the "Go Kiss A Moose" T-shirts on sale? Yes, but not the "I froze my buns in Alaska" ones. Out into the rain with what I did manage to get. The road on to Auke Bay is as black as the proverbial witch's heart - which is close to that of the average California attorney - and as it was when I first traveled it three months earlier at 2:30 a.m. after arrival in Juneau at the Auke Bay Ferry Terminal. The post office people don't know why some of my mail is being returned - bring the item in so that we can check on it. Will have to get the item from those that sent it on its' way to its' non-arrival. Wonder what else went astray? Letters from former loves? My winning notice from the Reader's Digest Sweepstakes? Back on the road to try to look at The World's Ugliest Boat which is for sale with three non-working motors. There may exist a real story. Find the road but the mud gets deeper so hold that dream for another day. Besides, can't see which house is yellow with brown trim and all the houses seem to have boats. On to the Nugget Department Store to see if they have the jeans. They remember the size that I mentioned last Saturday. (Only in Juneau do they still have clerks like that.) They still can't fill the order. Or provide the pie crust trimmer or the pie circle sheet. On down the mall to Gourmet Accents and another no. On the road again and aim the car between the fog line on the right and the Botts Dots on the left in the hope that Juneau will soon be there. Back to greetings from the landlord's Springer Spaniels, my rent-a-dogs, who come in to check things out. And I realize that with all the frustrations, every clerk and salesperson was pleasant. Which is definitely Juneau; perhaps we could market that quality and market it to the lower 48. Forecast for Wednesday is winds to 50 mph, five more and they will be over the speed limit, record high for the day 48 degrees, low minus five degrees, overnight 45 degrees, now 44 degrees. And the power is off at Thunder Mountain Mobil Home Park, sunset at 3:26 p.m.

THANKSGIVING DAY
1984

The day starts well, rains continuing but yesterday's winds have abated. Not my first holiday here but the first of stature, the ones that you pay attention to and that are time for family and friends. Except that the children/young adults are far from this area code as I know by the phone bill. Having had the opportunity of four possible places to partake of the festive bird, my choice was the church service and dinner to start at 2 p.m. twenty-two miles out the road at the Shrine of St. Therese. I am on the list for apple and pumpkin pies. So after a holiday (non-diet) breakfast, the dough making and apple slicing gets underway. By 11 a.m. the oven is heating and the winds are rising. The barge city up the channel looks adrift. The rent-a-dogs charge up through the rain from the beach, having a fine day. As I wonder what would happen to thousands of turkeys baking in local ovens if the power failed again today, I have a chance to find out. Which leaves two apple pies in limbo and the shells for pumpkin ones to be finished in the dim light through the kitchen windows. Do I really want to drive to the feast through all that wind and rain and back after sundown which comes about 3:30 p.m.? When what do my wondering ears hear but a phone that works in spite of all. And an offer to share oven space with a turkey coming in from near Lemon Creek to be roasted where the volts still flow. Also, if the church expedition is a wash, an invitation to join a family for dinner. Which is how I got to the home of friends of a friend and son and had another welcome to Juneau in true Alaskan hospitality. This after I learned that the road to the shrine was blocked by a tree, there was no power there and regrets were being phoned around. The now host family are long-time Alaskans and Juneauites and own a local business. The requisite coffee pot was on and kids and friends flowed in, out, and around. A no-sweat relaxed time where various hands joined in to get the meal on. Lots of good conversation, good food, and good dessert after the stuffing settled. I learn that most of the buildings on South Franklin Street are built on pilings, which might account for some of the leanings. The host left after dinner to check his building, which has a basement that is below high tide level at times. All the area was built on tailings from the A. J. Mine - as was a lot of Egan Drive. That drive has the tide flowing under it and is subject to shifting.

Friday is calm with the winds abated, an ideal day for the work crews to get out, inspect the damage, and make preliminary repairs. The storm came, it blew, it went. All in a matter of hours, though there was a day of windy expectation before its' denouement. What it left after a swift trip through Southeast was damage to the extent of some $2,000,000 for just Juneau; in dollars of damage per hour, it was a champion. The 95 MPH winds combined with a high tide undermined parts of Egan Drive. The State Department of Transportation facilities at the Subport now has a sinking concrete floor and a cracked roof truss. A National Guard truck parked there ended up off of the pier in the water. Marine Park downtown is loose from the shore and needs $500,000 of foundation work. A lot of the road signs along Egan Drive are bent to ground level - unique but hard to read from your car. Auke Bay and DeHart's Marina out that way are a vision of docks and boats that went floating and bumping in the wind. Uncle Fats, our local radio personality, was one of the owners who will have to raise his boat up from the depths. A lot of chain saws got extra duty as neighbor helped neighbor get the fallen trees cut into next year's firewood. Worst hit locally was Tenakee Springs, thirty miles to the Southwest, where seventeen of thirty houses in the waterfront community were undermined when pilings were pounded by drifting logs and debris. Yancy Derringer's, our local waterfront emporium of good food and spirits, must close for a few days to make repairs. But no one seems to be shaken up by the aftermath of Thanksgiving Day 1984:

it may or may not be twenty years till the next storm like this one. Trevor Davis, a long-time local historian, photographer, and writer has movies of the 1936 storm which make interesting fare for the TV news on the day after this storm. Now THERE was a storm. The Guv visits Tenakee Springs and makes promises which may help; they will rebuild in any event. Bullwinkle's Pizza Palace won't close down simply because their sign blew away. Perhaps the spirit of this region is the way people step forward to help others cut their trees, get to work on time, fall back to a holiday dinner at a different place, without damning the weather for interfering. After all, like bunions and head colds, it's just a fact of life and complaining about them is not going to cause a cure. So, go with the flow, or perhaps with the blow.

END TO NOVEMBER
NOVEMBER 29, 1984

Snow on the ground at last. Not much but enough to see the tracks of some small non-resident dog on the deck as I go out to start the car this morning. A warmup for the wagon while my coffee warms me. The walk along the elevated ramp out to the parking place and back gives me a preview of how to dress for the day, which hat for warmth or rain, perhaps boots for the walking. What seems in order now may not be after work. The last few days have held firm at a near freezing temperature, slidey pavement, no daytime street slush. And crystal clear at night. So much, in fact, that on my nightly descent to the sleeping level, I hesitate to turn on the lights down there. The darkened pine trees are the first filter of the city lights from across the channel as they reflect on the water. How to, in a sense, gather the sensation and save it to draw on over the years? Would a camera, even with all the electronic wizardry, ever really capture what the eye can see? Ansel Adams, where are you now? A view to share or to have to share at some future time. And during the day, after our current 8:17 a.m. sunrise, the sun advances up the channel and around the S.O.B., the mountaintops catch the first radiance and reflect it toward the town. Bluer than blue sky combined with Alpine-like vistas as seen from an office chair. Work stops while the panorama is imbibed. Yet it is not cold outside yet, only a bit below freezing with ice that stays on the roads and parking lots though downtown streets are slush to cross. The doorlocks and buttons on the windward side of the wagon tend to freeze. Which is why no one calls the police when a citizen is seen crouching next to a car door trying to light the car key with a Bic, cricket, or match. It is the only way short of brute force to gain entry into their vehicle. The thing to remember is to not put the hot key into your mouth while juggling match, hot key, and gloves. Or use the pocket-sized spray bottle of lock deicer but not by mistake as a breath freshener, especially when smoking. If frozen locks are not exclusive to Alaska, why did I not encounter them in other cold climes? Probably because the cars I owned in high school and college did not usually have functioning door locks, or in one case, even doors. Not an original equipment item on a '23 Ford panel truck originally belonging to the Meyer Brush and Broom Company of Kansas City, Kansas. The bonus to the winter pace here is a lower stress level, enjoy the coffee, don't worry, any lateness will be understood.

ADVENT OF DECEMBER
DECEMBER 2, 1984

Advent Sunday to we Episcopalians and others, the first Sunday of the new church year. Up at 6:30 a.m. after an early (for Sunday) waking in the darkness. An hour or more before sunrise. Lots of time before church and other sundry Sunday things to do. Start by finding the glasses. Turning on a light would be an intrusion on the view outside. From this lower level of the house, which is above a further drop in the land toward the channel, there are fewer branches on the trees toward the channel and the extreme low tide is evident. The pattern of city lights is more visible from this level, patterns of orange reflections on the water, the white of downtown Juneau, the red of the light on the roof of the Federal Building. A trek up the stairs, still in darkness, and a tour of the windows upstairs. The view toward the south from the living room is toward Douglas Highway aka North Douglas and about one hundred feet away from where the faithful Ford is parked next to the road, slightly covered with snow. There is a sloping gravel drive down from the road to the lower level of the house. It is too steep to consider using in winter but great for the landlord's kids to slide on in their plastic slider-type things and for the rent-a-dogs to charge over, though not at this early hour. An early car heads west on the road; what to do out that way so early, Eaglecrest or what? Continue my circle to the dining area where the view is northeast toward the city. Here it is higher than the ground level sleeping area one floor lower and the tree limbs are part of the pattern. On to the kitchen where out over the counter along the north wall a long window allows a view west and north. Lights of a car inbound on Egan Drive from the Valley. The barge city up the channel is dark - a floating mass bathed in the yellow light reflections. No running lights to warn boaters. A good in-house walking tour and, as I stand, I think of Saturday's walk at the Nugget Mall. So far I have not seen all of the malls here in as much detail as this one where everyone seems to go. While there may be individual loyalties to one mall or another, everyone ends up at the Nugget. Forget Fred Meyer as it is not a mall but an everything-in-one-store place, functional, efficient, and dollar-extraction friendly but without the personality of the Nugget Mall. Jordan Creek tries for class, Mendenhall is more neighborhood in nature, Grants Plaza and the Emporium each have a reason for being, but Nugget is the universal one. The day, after a "mano a mano" with a snowplow in the parking lot, was a seeking of sausage gravy over biscuits and under eggs as a start to the day of errands. What I sought was sold out to the early shoppers so I have hot cakes and eggs as a stand-in. Then out to the enclosed mall strolling area to find a few things - and what I find is a sea of Girl Scouts, Camp Fire Girls, Brownies, and their leaders who have set up camp to display and sell Christmas items that they have made. Moms and Dads are there to oversee the festivities. The candies are enticing but not really needed this early in the season. They would never last till the Day. Round tuits are a staple item at several of the locations. The wind whirlers in three sizes are a neat idea and would be a great gift for my favorite aunt if she was able to get outside to enjoy one. The log carriers of canvas and wood are very practical. I select a trio of reindeer made of clothes pins for the tree that isn't selected yet, but get them at the three for a dollar table rather than the $2.50 each place. Girls, you have to see what the competition is doing. And a spice rack for the favorite aunt - it helps with kitchen odors - as if the ones in her kitchen were ever other than pleasant. What I take with me as I head for the car is not so much the material items as the warmth of the sense of community that the sale shows. Last year at California's Montclair Plaza in Sunny Smogland the big deal on the indoor mall was a demonstration of a white Astroturf ski slope where hot doggers and snow bunnies can practice between weekends on real slopes. And arts and crafts items sold mainly by adults for the profit of adults. An ode to the true commercialization of the season. Here, in what people outside see as the frozen wasteland, it is a lot of kids sharing with love their troop projects that they have worked on over the past months. Which brings out a feeling that the traditional values of togetherness in a community are alive and well in Southeast. May all those Munchkins find full stockings on the Morning Of.

FIRST SERIOUS SNOW
DECEMBER 11-15, 1984

Monday morning off-to-work-we-go time introduces the winter's first snowfall of significance over our town and valley. Not the teasers of the past two months but real flakes that seem an inch or more in diameter as they float down past the fifth floor of the S.O.B. The seeming softness is lessened when driven by the brisk twenty-five mile-an-hour wind onto the sloggers along the street below. Beautiful stuff to watch from the workplace when one does not have to brush it off the car or drive too far through it. A time to choose footwear more for comfort than looks. Snowpacs with the three-piece suit are in local style. The fall continues all day, slows a bit around our 3 p.m. sunset, gains momentum again, and goes on through the night and most of Tuesday. The sight of snowplows in tandem on Egan Drive becomes as routine as the parade of snowblowers on the sidewalks. Each journey in the car involves clearing of three or four inches of new snow before starting out, a light cleaning at any intermediate stop, and a heavy brushing and scraping if the stop is very long. The wipers move mountains of the stuff from the glass but, when parking, can't come to rest because of the pileup. At least the mountains of wet snow are moved to the non-wiper area - where side vision is then blocked. Finally, after nearly thirty hours of non-stop falling, it ends as the temperature climbs to forty degrees and rain starts. This is evidenced by falling-from-trees snow showers when I walk to the road to say goodnight to a Tuesday dinner sharer. By Wednesday morning it has either halted completely or fallen back to regroup. At least the snow is without the minus thirty degrees reported in Fairbanks. Of course, as a result of the weather, an adjuster headed from Seattle to Juneau saw Yakutat twice and Cordova once before returning to Seattle to try another day. And there are concerns that the Guv. won't get back to town to head the reception line at the annual open house at the Governor's Mansion. But he gets into town as the snowfall's new start slows late in the day and I join the throng of state employees, families of state employees, other local citizens, and dignitaries who troop the line, eat the sumptuous goodies, and sip hot cider while finding out how much space there is in the place on the hill overlooking Juneau. The fact that at times cars have difficulty getting all the way to the top of the hill doesn't make it a bad place to live - and it is just a short stroll to the Capitol so the incumbent can pop home for lunch if he wants to. The shorter distances between places here become more understandable now: the getting there and back can be a real challenge every now and then. And it sure makes for less streets to plow. Maybe those urban planners who have spread Southern California all over the landscape could learn a bit by seeing the way we live here on the Frontier. I slog back down the hill, through the S.O.B., and to the parking lot where I can look back up to the ongoing reception scene before sliding homeward. On toward Thursday at 6:15 a.m. when Uncle Fats comes over the airwaves to advise of a change in the weather: the outlook is for rain late in the day and rising winds with gusts to fifty knots. Oh Happy Day. A relief of sorts from the snow for those who demand variety in their weather. And lower temperatures which will lead to ice abounding. Which makes a planned evening trip to the Valley uncertain. But the day brings snow instead of rain and light wind. So the trip to the Valley is easy; it is the trip back through blowing snow that makes for driving excitement. Wander with the other pilgrims through an unmarked wilderness populated by Broncos, Blazers, Mustangs, and similar beasts of the pavement. By Friday a.m. it is all quiet, back to ten degrees and frozen door locks and handles, which is the way the weekend goes. By Sunday sunshine is reflecting off the snow-covered mountains as we head for The Day, just over a week away.

CHRISTMAS IN SIGHT
DECEMBER 12-24, 1984

As my first official Christmas on the Last Frontier approaches, I try to keep some chaotic notes over the twelve days prior to The Day. My answer to the question of whether I will keep busy and avoid the remembrances of Christmases Past with negative nostalgia is that there is no time for any blue funk periods. The time turns out to be busier but less frantic than many such seasons in the Southland. Not doing everything at the last minute because now I have time to do otherwise may be the answer to the lower seasonal stress level.

The start of the season, after Advent at the church, was the December 12th reception and tour at the manse of the state's chief executive. He was "in" prior to leaving town for a minor eye operation after which he would recoup at his Palm Springs, California residence. Thus avoiding the cold part of December before returning for the legislative session. Thursday, the 13th was a singles group discussion on how to handle the feelings of being single at Christmas. With travel plans for my kids coming and going, there seems to be more joy and anticipation than with many non-singles. On the way back from the Valley not much time to think on what was said as the snowfall directed full attention to driving. The next day the One Who Is In Charge Of My Work left for his holiday giving me an extra gift of official papers to read for a few weeks. On the 15th, Saturday already, back to the Valley for a breakfast meeting and an early tour of the shops without yet buying things on the list. Plus deciding what to put on the list. What else for the kids when the major items won't fit in a suitcase anyway? Sunday is off to church plus off to the store with the groceries where the Bird is bought before the prices drop. A frozen fellow at 14.3 pounds as the fresh ones are all spoken for. Then out to the Nugget Mall for a gift for myself and the Bird - a roasting pan of sufficient size if Bird's wings are tied up instead of locked under as the book directs. And to buy gifts to mail out before the last reasonable flight day. Here, it can go by air if the planes don't miss us for a day or so. Also spend some time looking for a bed for the spare room so Daughter won't have to sleep on the floor during her visit; the place where the bed is for sale is a story in itself. Apparently it was an attempted eviction by trying to sell the tenant's bed. And end the day by learning that the Crèche is out of storage and will be sent in time for Christmas. Thereby keeping a family tradition.

COUNTING DOWN
MONDAY, DECEMBER 17, 1984

The day starts with a trip to the dentist, not primarily to wish him season's greetings. And is followed after work by an effort to find a parking spot downtown so that the sleds can be picked up. Two are for here and two for small friends in Fairbanks. I find that our local version of "no room at the inn" is finding no place to park downtown. At least no place within a block of the hardware store, not even a loading zone. Apparently a lot of others are also finally shopping. So the guy in the suit and overcoat totes four sleds a block to where the car was finally parked with its' one operating door. Stuff the sleds in over the front seat back and then drive off holding the door shut as it won't latch. Hide the big sleds and then label the small ones for the aerial run to the Interior.

Thursday, a day of more snow, so what's new is when I lose the house key in the snow on the way back from lunch and have to call the landlord to get a new one. Which I get after I lose a car key belonging to a friend while trying to move a VW from the street before it becomes impounded by the city authorities. The lack of rear wheel support on one side due to an advanced case of Juneau body makes the task impossible. Even the Ford can't push the VW on snow. This is a day when I have already picked up new glasses, stood in a long line at the post office, and decided not to buy the bed I was to buy because the evicted tenant answered the phone when I called about picking it up. On to Wednesday and another trip to the post office where twelve people line up in an area the size of a walk-in closet. It is cheery, anyway. The snow melts as I drive out to the Auke Bay P.O. box (two times in a post office in one day in the holiday season?), then to Alaska Air Lines Air Freight for a package where I learn that they close at 5:30 and to Western Air Lines where the sleds are shipped north. All these things after the 6:45 a.m. call letting me know that the Crèche was on the way. Thursday is a day of respite as it is only work, the Crèche pickup, caroling (after work) at the local hospital, and coffee with friends afterwards. Work includes a reception given by our Commissioner, which is a sort of requirement of the season to let us all know that our efforts are appreciated. As we in the office had already taken a cake up to the people in Word Processing, they having sent us cookie goodies earlier, we were in the spirit anyway. I even had time earlier in the day to pick up items from the Forest Service so the arriving kids would learn about Juneau and where trees can be cut legally.

Friday, December 21, and the day that Daughter Kate is to arrive. I attend an early potluck dinner and head for the airport. En route I find that Western Airlines has decided to go directly to Fairbanks without even flying by Juneau to see if the airport lights are on. A number of calls later finally reveals that the flight got to Fairbanks, which is a fair distance from Juneau, that Daughter did not elect to spend the night at airline expense in Seattle, and that therefore she is a guest at the Fairbanks Airport where she spends the night in the closed terminal. And leaves on a flight at some early hour so that I can meet her at 8:30 Saturday morning. After which I berate the airline for allowing an underage passenger to stay overnight in the airport. Then she is given the grand tour of Auke Bay, Nugget Mall, Fred Meyer, and downtown Juneau before we borrow a bed for her. Then we head back to pick up Son at 8 p.m. We leave the house with all the wagon doors working, lose two to freezing by the time we stop at Fred Meyer, lose the other two while trying to stop for hot chocolate at McDonald's where we exit and enter the car by a window, the exit scene being repeated at the airport. The tailgate consents to open so we are now able to crawl in from that area after Son John arrives. Which brings us all together as Sunday dawns. There is appropriate snow falling on Sunday morn as we head for church so that Juneau is seen in a fairly normal configuration. The afternoon is spent donning camera and outdoor gear as we head out North Douglas Road to find a suitable Christmas tree, which is cut down by John and hauled home by Ford. Then out to find a tree stand and to introduce John to the stores I had introduced Kate to the day before.

The Day before the Day was work of sorts till 3 p.m., followed by last minute shopping, buying of used chairs at a home in Auke Bay (like the typical thing to do on the Eve is to pick up six used chairs for Christmas sitting), deliver ingredients to the aspic and pie maker for the Dinner, deliver the forgotten plates to the same place, wrap gifts, prepare a dinner for the kids and then off to sing at the 11 p.m. service. After which Santa could not get down the stovepipe so the old rascal had to leave the sleds on the deck in the snow. Tiny Tim would have certainly approved of the wood fire, hot chocolate and family gift openings as new snow drifted past the windows. And a time of new things for our book of remembrances.

COUNTING DOWN TO 1985
DECEMBER 28, 1984

Now comes Nadir time in the North, the nub of the year, post-Christmas, pre-New Year, with a gangplank fever of sorts to get into the New Year. Winter is now officially here as the days haltingly become longer, some daylight at 3:30 in the afternoon but 4:30 quitting time is still in darkness. The pre-Christmas snow is still all around us, though part of it thawed during one very brief warm spell leading to slush which now is still frozen on the roadways. Slip and slide along and wonder what magical skills allow the more daring drivers to pass on the thick ice coating. The Juneau temperature report sounds more like a state-wide pattern as the range is from sixteen degrees downtown at 6:30 a.m. to ten degrees out at Fritz Cove to minus five degrees on the Back Loop Road. With Thursday predictions of Taku winds that will cause the wind chill factor in open areas to be a Fairbanks-like minus thirty degrees. Weather is more than a subject for casual conversation here as so much of what we do and how we survive is based on an awareness of what is coming or going weather-wise. At least I have one door on the wagon that functions allowing entry and exit other than by window. I now carry bungee/shock cords in the car to secure any door that opens but won't re-latch. Also a length of line/rope to keep the tailgate from swinging open now that I have gotten it unstuck by using a small pry bar. My current companions in this battle with nature are the college freshman son and the high school junior daughter here for the holidays from Minnesota and Montana respectively. They are good sports about the chill spell here but wonder why locks don't freeze where they live. They found Cope Park Friday morning but sled tryouts were called off due to the frigid air. A retreat to wood stove and hot chocolate seemed to make more sense. About the same time, my stroll downtown on minor errands found the rising wind to be notice to pull the wool hat over the ears or risk frost damage. Thursday night was not quite as cool but the departure on a drive to the Valley for a potluck was delayed while trying to get the wagon to move forward on the ice of the parking area and on to the road. This was finally accomplished by pushing, rocking, and uttering words of frustration, which were accompanied by the odor of snow tires warming the ice. There are better ways to exercise.

Life indoors seems conditioned to use of the wood stove and those indoor family activities done most everywhere except that here boots, coats, hats and gloves are hung and slung in abundance near the door.

The off-repeated daily ritual includes donning part of the pile to journey out into the darkness to see if the wagon is still alive. So far all is well out next to the road where it winters. A last-thing-at-night warmup is done to help that wellness. Which is a good time to look at the beauty of the stars in the crystal clearness of the night sky. The Big Dipper seems like a next door neighbor as I reflect on the lessons learned in the midst of the first full winter here. Such as to not park the wagon on ice with the rear wheels lower than the front wheels if one intends to drive out before the thaw. And I have learned to appreciate not having the minus thirty degrees and four feet of snow that Fairbanks has. I also know that the beauty around our town makes the harsh weather tolerable as does the warmth of the people here. As the last days of a good year wind down, there are remembrances of other holiday seasons, other places and other friends and of family times. This one has been special because of having the kids here during my first season so far from the prior life. Yet it is tinged with the realization that before long they will be families of their own and Dad will either have to travel outside or pay more homage to the phone company. My life and my friends are here now and what I will do in the future will be centered here. So, kids, your White Christmas is here when you want it. And I prepare to usher the well-used year out, store away the events therein, and see what circa 1985 has in store for me. With kids, health, a working car, and the fishing season coming up, Taku winds are just a minor fact of life.

IN TO 1985

JANUARY 5, 1985

Saturday, January 5, 1985, the first day with that name in the New Year. The rains of the past three days have abated leaving mottled snow on the slope toward the channel. As seen in the dawn light at 8:10 a.m. while I contemplate the needs of the day in re errands and fun things and map out what and when. Some must do items and others if time and ambition allow. Like giving the Wagon a chance to enjoy 10/30 oil for a change now that winter is past the cold part, hopefully. First, though, there is an errant Christmas package from The Children's Mother for The Children, at the Douglas Post Office, if that is where it is. The Yellow Slip Leaver forgot to designate. If not there, try the Main Post Office except that it closes on Saturdays, only the little guys at the branches don't get Saturday off. I and kids and The Mother have been wondering what happened to this package. Apparently when its' traveling companion came, there was (a first) yellow notice slip which was assumed to be for the box that was delivered next door (left there). Why one package was left and one was not is one of those eternal mysteries, post office type, that may never be answered during this earthly pilgrimage. So, Daughter Kate having flown Western Airlines out on the winds of Wednesday, Son John and I head out. The first stop indicates that the Douglas Post Office is not open at 9 a.m.. Out to the Big Boy in the Nugget Mall for sausage gravy over biscuits and under eggs after the waitress sits down with us to take John's order as it is lengthy. On to a meeting of sorts to discuss what can be done to involve the single's children in some phases of our group. On to the Auke Bay P.O. to check for bills and letters, then further out the road to visit the Shrine of St. Therese and to show Son how it is as the road starts to run out. The sun of the distant snowy peaks across the water is enjoyed by both. Back to Fred Meyer for son's sundries as he leaves Monday. Check the Douglas P.O., find it open and also find that the package is at the big post office. And the last stop is Foodland, where the birds winter on the roof, for the week's rations. Save for another day the oil change and the return of the bed borrowed for Daughter. Do the dinner menu which includes salad for three for John before relaxing in my "study" and thinking of the things to be done - aside from the employment that pays the freight - over the next few months. Before fishing starts in a serious way. It is enrollment time at UA - Juneau and there is a plethora of goodies in the class listings. The class on survival sounds like something every Urban Sourdough should have if there is any plan to go past the city boundaries - or even to some places within them. The class conflicts with the Thursday night meeting and Hill Street Blues which is double jeopardy. A choice is made even more difficult as the community school schedule is also out and, considering other community activities, makes the selection process even more agonizing. The cooking class that I am to teach and the writing class will have to be made part of the equation. An interesting puzzle when there is also an exercise program, plays, lectures, and civic functions to possibly attend. Our town of 26,000, though isolated by water and mountains, has the uniqueness of offering more to do than one can. Pick and choose and try to save time for self, family, and friends. And for the fish that wait and for seeing the rest of the state. A real Alaska-size challenge. While not forgetting to look up and around as you go. The pitfall to avoid is becoming so enmeshed that time is not taken to realize how fully He Who Created All This Blessed Southeast with evidence of His Majesty. Perhaps when that task was underway, all the best parts were stored here - and then found too large or too numerous to be moved elsewhere. Which may be why Texas didn't get any of the good pieces.

RAINY DAYS ARE HERE AGAIN
JANUARY 11, 1985

The year starts well with a continuing heat wave as daily temperatures soar up to the low forties. So far it has rained every day this year, which aptly justifies the T-shirt legend "Welcome To The Juneau Rain Festival - January 1, 1985 to December 31, 1985." I receive a letter from a friend in Southern California and read about sun tan efforts undertaken on New Year's Day and the care needed to get equal burning on all exposed areas. No such problem here in Juneau. The challenge in these parts is how to get equal rust on all sides while exposed to the Juneau Sunshine. While moving often enough to avoid growing of green mold on the non-exposed parts. Suntan oil is light sewing machine grade to control the volume of rust: sun blocker is ten to forty weight oil matched to the temperature and rain fall amount. At least there are no long range problems with wrinkles due to excess exposure to the sun: chill blains maybe, but not wrinkles.

This is also apparently the season for potlucks and standup lunches and dinners. Sort of a mini-season attached to the Christmas Season and thereafter until Lent approaches. The series started with a pre-

Christmas potluck on December 21st for members of a church-related group. A service and meal and fellowship from which I left early for daughter's non-arrival at the airport. Then the Singles Again group had a December 27th post-Christmas dinner parade of leftovers potluck to pool and relegate to leftover heaven the feast day leavings. Which was followed by a December 30th church potluck to bring together town and valley members of the parish who had been rained and winded out of a Thanksgiving Day turkey sharing. The three sit-downs prior to New Year's were joined by a last minute bring-what-you-can on The Last Evening Of The Year. After which all was quiet on the food front until January 10th, when favorite snacks/hot dishes were gathered by the singles to add to a farewell for Father Rudy, the advisor for the group. Not a full potluck, but enough food taken in while standing to negate later dinner desires. Which was the last eating outing till the next day when a retirement fete for a long-time employee of the Department of Administration was the noon-hour festivity. Now there is a down-time till the 27th when the parish annual meeting will be preceded by a potluck. Which will be the next-to-last in the seasonal series; the singles hold one more on the 31st. That should be sit down and will give an opportunity to start a new month with self-promises of now starting the diet that was contemplated for a month earlier. At least, as a result of the State outing, I got to a formal potluck where the good plastic forks were used, the napkins were of a superior quality, and I learned more about How The State Works. Having never met the guest of honor, but feeling that such a detail should not keep me from attending, I did find out who it was - the pleasant gentleman seen in the halls and elevators - and found that the Commissioner is allowed to step eight to ten places ahead in line without objections and that the people I don't know in the department seem very nice. Maybe if I last till retirement, I will know more of them. At least I did chat with one lady as we struggled to fill top-heavy plates of nominal strength. And now know that I am not the only ex-freeway traveler who left the smoggy Basin de Los Angeles to head north. No fear of an invasion, however, as long as the publicity people keep sending out those stories about mosquitoes the size of Piper Cubs and how cold it is in Fairbanks.

THE SESSION SEASON
JANUARY 16, 1985

The first harbingers of the Legislative Session that started with a flurry of media concentration last Monday in Our Town, The State Capitol, were the new faces at the Church and some expensive automobiles seen tooling up and down Egan Drive. The new faces are, in general, accompanied by suit and tie which in and of itself is not unusual attire at an Episcopal service. Except for the celebrant. However, by this stage of the winter season, most of the regulars have retreated to more practical attire to go with the snow boots and/or Juneau Tennies. A sport coat and shirt and tie is the usual high water mark of sartorial splendor these days. As for cars, there is a white Cadillac El Dorado convertible, the one that was last made in 1976 till the recent revival of ragtops, which has been spotted near the S.O.B. and on Egan Drive. Convertibles, while not unknown here, are rare except when the convertible status is the result of upper level rust. And there has been a reported spotting of two Lincolns, a Town Car and a Continental Sedan, not seen before on the Town to Valley Freeway. Perhaps the polls are bringing their luxury cars to cruise the extensive forty mile Juneau road system during breaks in the session. With a tank of gas and an hour or so to spare, all the paved main roads can be traveled. The importers of these fine machines are apparently concerned more with the need for comfort than the needs of the urban Juneauite's daily encounter with rain, snow, and mud. Then, after leaving the parking lot, the fun starts. I doubt whether any of the legislators are too concerned with hauling firewood, fishing tackle, fish, dead deer or doing any of the other chores that Juneau cars are accustomed to.

The pace of the town has quickened a bit with the session underway. Much of the evening news is coverage of the day's events at the Capitol, which is out the back door of the S.O.B. The local Public Broadcasting Corporation station no longer has a newscast, since when two of the three-person staff were left after the third person resigned and then one more left, the staff of one was too small to carry on. Being so close to government in motion is a new experience. It's government in action all around at close range as the City/Borough Assembly meets just down the hill from the Capitol. A rare chance to see that lawmakers are mortals also. And they will be amongst us until the tourist season starts.

CAKE TIME
JANUARY 19, 1985

Somehow, even with the distances involved, Birthday Week went off fairly well this year. A matter of adjustment to the celebrants being in three different places for the first time since the kids and their male parent decided to celebrate all their birthdays in one week. After the original arrival of the children, John a day before Dad's thirty-fourth celebration, and Katherine three days after his thirty-sixth, which solved what to give him as a gift in those years, we were able to split one cake in addition to any individual parties. Since the segregation of the family started a few years ago, John has celebrated two at home in San Diego and Upland, and two away, in Fairbanks and in Montana. Kate has been at home until this year. Including last year's Sweet Sixteen surprise party to which Dad unwittingly invited three boys she was interested in. I didn't know that she would open the gift of "dainties" from an honorary auntie in front of the crowd. A tradition of the week has been to attend Church together and to ambush the priest when he calls for those who have birthdays to come forward to put a penny for each year in the cup. At that juncture, all three of us would step up. Surprise. This year they are both away so I dropped the pennies per year in the receptacle - using two full rolls of pennies even though the total was somewhat less than one hundred years. John called on Sunday and we exchanged birthday wishes. His Mother called on Monday and Kate called on the fifteenth as I was thinking about how the days are increasing into more years. A cake at the office with friends was the day's celebration. Greeting cards from several of the singles made the transition in age and place of celebration go easier. And cards from friends in Southern California and a letter from one were received. So it was a nice day, if not a landmark year such as forty or fifty. Only a fleeting thought that a time warp seems to making the decades shorter. Last year the proud parent of kids sixteen and eighteen, next year eighteen and twenty. And me facing a thirty-fifth high school reunion with no desire to travel and see those elderly folks I attended school with. If life begins at forty, I am now thirteen years old and enjoying every minute if it.

SUPER BOWL SUNDAY
JANUARY 20, 1985

This Super Bowl Sunday is a long way from Number One when we - spouse, infant son who is now as old as the series, and me, were living in Chico, Northern California. My job at the time was as a trainee for General Adjustment Bureau, now known as GAB Services. A fact that I remember because part of that Sunday was spent not watching the birth of a new American January rite, but instead looking for VW tracks in the Feather River Canyon north of Oroville. Friends from Sacramento, the Riethers, had journeyed into the Far Country for the weekend. Eggs Benedict were on tap for lunch but my first interest was to confirm if possible that an insured's VW had really left the road next to the river and became a floating bug on the turbulent waters. The driver had reported that he had bailed out of the bug after swerving to avoid a rock in the roadway, becoming airborne for a while, and then realizing that he was in a sinking car. As he swam to shore he could see the car with lights on floating toward a power plant intake screen. Better car than him. So, with visitor, I took my company car up toward Bullard's Bar and spent the morning finding and interviewing local residents in the mountainous area. We never did find any witnesses or skid marks but had a great time tromping around in the remote villages. A number of Super Bowls have passed since that one, some with parties, some without. The current one, San Francisco v. Miami, is my first one viewed in Alaska and the one that spaghetti was involved in. Which is to say that the Wednesday before I had made an abundance of spaghetti sauce in my Dutch Oven. After dinner I realized that I would have to learn to love spaghetti for a long time to be able to use up the sauce supply. Or fill the freezer or feed people. So, on Thursday I suggested to Rick of the deer cutting project that perhaps a Super Bowl party might be a way to use up the sauce. He agreed and then let the lady he intends to marry know that she was going to host a party, with his help of course. Which lead to impromptu telling of others and to game watching with a small group plus kids with subsequent spaghetti eating along with world's largest one-dish salad for the watchers. Good conversation made the lack of game action and a well-earned San Francisco victory not too important. Being there with friends was more important; they are part of my future here.

THE COMMITTEE
JANUARY 22, 1985

Having been neither for nor against Nimbus, a local work of greenish metal sculpture until recently situated near the state capitol, yet having tried to fuel the flames of local debate by letters to the editor and the writing of a Nimbus poem, I could not sit at home when the appointed committee charged with finding a replacement for Nimbus and a new site for the displaced art object scheduled a public hearing on the issues.

Naturally, the meeting was in the courthouse adjacent to where Nimbus had been but no longer was. Mayor Fran, a state representative, a veteran's group spokesman, an arts group person, and a judge made up the committee. The judge was the only member who under normal circumstances would be in the courtroom and therefore seemed right at home. Fifty or more local people also attended and were invited to sign a list if they wished to speak. After the issues and alternatives were presented, the citizens were allowed to step up and give a maximum three minute statement. The content and variety of the opinions expressed showed a great deal of thought, interest and concern with a great deal of originality. After all the input needed for making a recommendation was heard and after the politicians in the audience had their say, the meeting adjourned. Democracy in action after the removal of Nimbus by executive fiat. But not one raised voice at the meeting, no emotional outbursts, pro or con. It was a dignified meeting with only one politician trying to inject any humor. My reaction to all this is that they (the citizens and the committee) are all taking this a bit too seriously. They are not having fun as they go about the task. Not that any such situation does not require much thought and consideration and doing what is artistically sound; the not doing of those things may have led to the present dilemma. And we should honor our veterans and display Alaska art. But it is almost like we are trying too hard to show that in the shadow of the Capitol, we are no longer frontier persons with the smell of wood smoke clinging to our animal skin garb and are just in from the Bush. We seem to be so intent on being a model city in a model state that we forget that this is Alaska, last real refuge of the individualist. Where one can make a living fishing if possessed of enough points to qualify for a permit. Where one can mine for a living if one can get to the mine past all the many regulations that block the path. Where timber is abundant yet subject to regulations that can't be cut through with the biggest chainsaw. I can imagine that in the recent past, if a Nimbus was objected to, it might well have disappeared without any executive direction, never to be seen again except perhaps at a very low tide. Which makes me wonder whether there might be some correlation between the high ratio of college degrees in the local population and the courtly demeanor with which really serious problems like Nimbus are considered. If we all try hard enough, we can really make the Great Land into one just like the place we left behind to come here. And then spend our declining years muttering about whatever happened to the Real Alaska.

THE BOAT
JANUARY 26, 27, 1985

Aside from the ownership of an oversized FWD pickup with a gun rack, there is one possession that seems common to all new and most long-time Alaskans. That is the accouterment that every home seems to have in the driveway, at the side of the house, or lurking nearby in the street or road. Or maybe a trailer for the one that is in the water somewhere. The custom of boat ownership is especially noticeable here in Southeast where King Salmon reigns along with his kin. And the lack of roads makes travel by boat or air as usual as driving is elsewhere.

As a confirmed dabbler in the art of fishing and having had both power and sailboats in the warmer waters of California, I had some thoughts of buying a boat before the 1985 fishing season got underway. Nothing major, just something to get out where the line won't snag and where the action is. Also to use to get over to the islands near here where the bears hang out. So when I was offered a boat and trailer for $49.50, my interest was raised even though I thought there might be a catch other than fish. Which turned out to be some minor hull problems arising from rocks which had led to a race to shore as the boat filled with water. I envisioned a pile of warped aluminum and getting my money back from sale of the trailer so I made the deal sight unseen. The move was a good one as I found the 16' Gamefisher, which now holds water in my driveway, can be fixed. With repairs and an engine, I will be ready for spring.

Of course the seller needed room for his next boat which is a 21' Glassply that only needs to be re-powered. That will be done by fiber glassing over the jet drive ports and installing an outboard motor, thereby gaining fishing room where the engine was. Two weeks ago I helped get the boat off blocks and on to a trailer to take to his house. A week ago we tried to put it into his garage so that work could start. Even with the wheels off and the trailer on the ground, the boat was two inches too high for the passage through the door. Yesterday we tried again. The moving crew, after coffee, left the boat and went in search of a cement drill, shopped for eyebolts to put in the rear garage floor, and checked three places before finding a come-a-long. Then we put the bolts in the floor, rigged chains, and used the come-a-long to pull the boat off the trailer and into the garage. Where it now sits waiting for the work. April 1 is the date set for the reverse process, after which the repairs will be checked by placing the boat into the water. Some future buyer of the house may wonder why there are eyebolts in the garage floor near the freezer.

PERSPECTIVE
JANUARY 29, 1985

Now I have over five months of settling into the not-so-new-anymore life here and feel that it is time to reflect on what brought me to the North. Whether it was a seeking of new horizons, the discarding of an old skin and the growing of a new one in a sense, or, most likely, a fulfillment of parts of long unheeded dreams. Perhaps some of each of them with dreams in the lead.

To a larger extent than most of us realize or are willing to admit, we do live lives of dreams tempered by reality. What we want in our innermost being over the whole earthly journey, the big dream as opposed to the short range. "My dream is to be happy" is the common response as opposed to the short range dream of a new car or of next year's journey to an island paradise. The "American Dream" of growing up, raising a family, ultimate retirement and going out with dignity and no pain. Yet it comes to a point where the dreams are sublimated by the very acts taken in pursuit of them. Earn the way to the ultimate hope and perhaps in the end not reaching the goal as a result of the effort or looking back and saying "It might have been."

These concepts came home to roost as a result of two recent events. I stumbled across a book called "A Dreamer's Log Cabin" by Laurie Shepherd last Saturday at The Nugget Mall. And read it all at one sitting. Which is a thing I normally do only with books by John D. McDonald or Ernest K. Gann. And the next day during a church discussion, one person expressed a dream of living in Europe where a job was available - except for the apparent real reluctance to venture forth from the known and reasonably secure. Perhaps an intelligent decision not to take the risk, but at what cost? The dream of Laurie Shepherd, schoolteacher, educated and of apparent sound mind, was to build and live in a remote log cabin with a minimum of amenities and minimal needs from urban society. (Would she have enjoyed it as much if there were not the relief valves of occasional trips to the city for shower and shampoo and musical events?) And she does not lack for human contact with family and friends. Yet has isolation. Time to know one's self. Her lifestyle and those reported on in a recent issue of Time about people in the more remote parts of Idaho are not a new wave. There have always been those who prefer some distance from the mainstream. An acknowledgment that not all in urban society appeals to all. Yet mankind cannot retreat en masse to a Walden. We need those who march to the universal drummer to keep the wheels turning at an ever faster rate ere the whole castle tumbles down. And most of us most of our lives are realistically prevented by self or societal needs from exercising the initiative to realize our dreams till at last the financial means may exist but the physical limitations limit. Seduced by indoor plumbing, central heat and the daily routines, the dreamer sees little hope of ever doing more than fantasizing, or thinking only of wishes that never will be.

Somehow, though, there will always be those who do manage to live their dreams to a degree, if not totally. If not to the extent of fully risking, embarking to the place where the cabin will be, taking the job in Europe, at least dusting off of the dream and perhaps finding a partial fulfillment. If one is financially able, happens to be at a time of transition, out of school, out of the last job, at the end of a relationship, at last has the kids away in college, and if not controlled by society and stability, (church, bowling league, fishing season), then perhaps a decision will be made to risk, to accept the challenge. This is what I want to do. How it will be done is less crucial than simply doing.

And of course I am frustrated that after taking the first step of my dream of a life on The Last Frontier, I need my job to keep on toward the rest of the dream. And I do not have all the time I want to read and reflect and write and learn. So I now pledge to myself to embark on the rest of the dream. To have time to be with friends and with myself. To love many people and perhaps, if God wills it, to be in love again. And to enjoy the community of mankind and of myself. To commune in the truest sense of the word. To take time to enjoy and acknowledge the wonders that are all around me. To buy the lot not too far from town, build my space with room for those who come along. To owe nothing except the property tax, the phone company, and the electric company if I use some of their power. To be able to be independent to whatever extent I choose. And to be by myself when I want to be but never alone. And to know that when this dream is accomplished, there will be another one.

MY VENERABLE FRIEND
FEBRUARY 1, 1985

A central character in the Alaskan venturing is my friend of a special sort over the past four years. That being my venerable, sort of green, 1970 Ford Country Squire wagon, the ten passenger version with a ravenous-for-fuel 390 cubic inch iron heart. The duly sanctioned given name is the Tuna Boat, a sobriquet given when the then unused but used wagon was on loan to a friend in Upland whose own car was in for fender cosmetics arising from not stopping as fast as a preceding car. During the transition from an economy car to one that is grossly otherwise, the friend learned that "E" on the gas gauge is for empty, not "enough." Pushing 3,600 pounds of Ford off of the freeway single-handed is not as easy as Toyota pushing. Later, in answer to a phone call for his mother, the lady's son replied that she was outside washing the Tuna Boat. A name was thereby bestowed on the resident example of how big and solid a car could be built before the era of multiple smog devices and fuel shortages.

My first meeting with the wagon was in late 1981 after a leased Datsun ran out of lease and was bought by my sister for Fairbanks use. Knowing that I was without wheels and that city life without a car is difficult, a client who was in the business of marketing automobiles having former owners offered to provide me a car in lieu of a monthly retainer. Which led to a series of encounters with cars on the way through his lot. The white Lincoln Continental was superb except for the reluctance of the electric windows to operate down when driving or up when parking. And taking the dogs to the beach was not good for the white leather interior. The Chevy Nova had headlights that only worked during daylight. Then came the Ford. Which ran, had working windows - even if the knobs were gone, and lights. Except for a time when water pump failure led to head gasket syndrome, it has been a faithful companion to my wanderings. Except for the time the transmission retired. It did have a year of vacation in Upland while I flirted with company-furnished cars. During which time it was used by a San Diego family and the Upland friend. When Alaska became more certain, I embarked on a Ford fixing campaign. That led to new front tires, front suspension overhaul, and those efforts needed to keep the engine temperature at a reasonable level. The last was my only real concern in taking The Road North in the wagon. And which heat level has not been off the peg since getting here. So I am blessed with a Southern California car turned Juneauite that has doors that close - and even freeze shut after closing- and that has started every day except when I once threatened to park at the airport for three days while on a trip. A wagon that cruises Egan Drive at a stately 55 miles an hour in comfort, has room for the fishing gear or a six-foot hide-a-bed, and can be worked on at home. Which is a financial advantage here where the mechanics charge as much as a Lower 48 plumber. It's the ideal car to be in Alaska with.

FOG
FEBRUARY 2, 1985

Saturday early a.m. after a busy Friday of office preparation for the semi-annual trek to Anchorage to review the work of our outside adjusting firms. The fog outside the residence makes for some doubt as to whether the trip will take place. The current lack of active precipitation is welcome as yesterday's newspaper (our Sunday paper which comes along on Friday) made official what was already obvious. There was rain every day in January in Juneau. Granted that one day had only a trace of measurable moisture somewhere in the hinterlands of this largest city (in area) in the whole U.S.A. The National Weather Service, keeper of such vital statistics, reports that a generous 15.35 inches of rain fell downtown during the month. Of course this is a whole .2 inch less than the all-time record set in 1949. This failure to set a new record downtown is not a total loss for those who glory in new rainfall records locally. The 10.13 inches out at the airport near the Fred Meyer store did set a new record. We usually average 6.89 in town and 3.69 at the airport for the period. Do we get extra credit for doubling the downtown average and tripling the airport average? At least we didn't have to contend with those above average yields in the area of snowfall, which was only one-third of the norm, or temperature which was 36.6 degrees most of the time rather than the 21.8 degrees which it generally averages in the first month of the year. We even basked in a day of 47 degree temperature, a new high for the date. My recap of all these important figures is made as I note that the fog or low clouds block the view of the channel and the city lights. A nice study, however, of the trees against the opaque background. The temperature seems to be declining as the fog closes in. It is nice to know that the daylight part of our day is getting longer as two hours and twelve minutes will be added this month. Nice to have a false light of sorts while driving to work just before 8 a.m. Not quite time yet to retire the winter garb, just the first realization that winter has started to yield to the next season. Not without a few further fights, however.

FURTHER NORTH
FEBRUARY 4-6, 1985

Monday in the too-early a.m. as Alaska Airlines Flight 73 heads for Anchorage where the semi-annual audit of contract adjusters is to be conducted. My second time on this junket so I am no longer a novice. Saturday, while at the Nugget Mall, I stopped at the Alaska Airlines ticket office and learned that the flights were having the usual seasonal problems of not being able to consistently get in and out of our town. Your plane has to get here before it can leave with you aboard. Sunday at 10 p.m. I called to reconfirm and found that one flight was in and one was on final approach. Pack and hope. Call for a cab to come at 6 a.m. as the Ford dislikes staying alone at the airport parking lot for more than a few minutes. Up, after a fashion, at 5 a.m., which should be sufficient time to do the necessaries and also pack what I didn't the night before and to have coffee. Run out of time for the coffee before stepping out the door and into several inches of new snow on the deck and more snow/rain plopping down in clumps. The cab and driver are waiting in the roadway, which is not too safe a spot. We get underway after the driver puts the shift lever back in where it had fallen from. The driver has qualms about driving on snow. What is he doing in Alaska? Somehow we get to the airport, perhaps aided by my efforts to calm the nervous driver. At least the lights are not going on and off as was the situation the last time this cab company took me out here. Off the ground and up to 35,000 feet and via Yakutat and Cordova to Anchorage. Darkness for a while, then the saw-toothed ridges of the mountains start to emerge in endless miles of stark majesty rearing upward in a soft crimson-hued dawn. Some of the lower valley floors are dark and seem snowless in vivid contrast to the whiteness of the peaks. Seeing the vastness from on high, one wonders how this land was ever settled. The parts tamed to a degree by we interlopers are such a minute part of the total. As I wonder how a land traveler would ever find a way through the wilderness, we cross over one more ridge and Anchorage looms as a sea of lights. Not yet the size of Los Angeles but very large. A turn over Cook Inlet - the one-quarter mile visibility announced earlier is much greater now - and we are ground-bound again. Hard snow on the pavement is a change of pace from the month of rain in Juneau. The nine hundred miles of possible flight further into the state is a reminder of how big Alaska is. That distance would bring us to the north state boundary at the Bering Sea. And we were not at the south boundary when exiting Juneau. The contrast is also noted in the time daylight emerges. Now, en route to work in Juneau at 7:45 a.m., there is less than total darkness. That stage arrives up here in Anchorage about 8:30. And on to the day of file reviews.

Tuesday starts a bit later than expected because of delays in chipping the ice off of the windows of the rental car after finding the rental's scraper brush, which then broke before the task was done. We Alaskans become very knowledgeable in selecting the better brands of ice scrapers. Some are sturdy and have good edges; some are cheap and don't cut the ice. Anchorage is a nice place to visit, to stroll through the J.C. Penney store after work, visit a large book store where they still don't have what you want, but for living, Juneau is the place. Anchorage, as a city, is just that. A large one in population, but Juneau has it and all U.S. cities topped for actual area. My quasi-resentment toward Anchorage is more a state of mind than a bona fide complaint. I can live and survive in a big city or not, on the Last Frontier or not. And opt not to be where the sprawl and the traffic and the distances govern daily life. Anchorage is very much Alaska, adjacent to the drawing cards of the state. My own druthers are to be in a smaller place where the attractions are closer at hand, not a long drive through the clutter of housing tracts and burger outlets that I left behind. In Juneau, there are no antelope at play, but the deer and bear are within hiking distance. And the fish are literally just out the door and off to the beach. Yet close to work and amenities. So the three-day sojourn is completed, stops made at a few stores to get what you can't in Juneau, and under a full moon and clear skies, back to Southeast and Juneau. Familiar faces on the airplane, a smooth flight, and glad to be back to the routine till the next trip out.

LOOKING BACK AND FORWARD
FEBRUARY 10, 1985

A Sunday where at a church discussion it is learned that none of the group are originally from here, that all are apparently happy being here in Juneau, within reason, and that there is a great deal of similarity in the reasons for not being where they were. Which reasons I seem to equate with my own for not being back in Kansas.

So why do many people leave the hometown, state, ties of the immediate family, and strike out on their own? Aside from forces of economic necessity, some unseen innate motivation surely must act on the individual. While this is not a new phenomena, there has been and still is in many lives a certain tendency to stick close to what is known, to take a minimum of risk. The village-town-city where one is "known" for better or worse, where one can rely on the known from season to season. Even to knowing where the ultimate planting place would be. And marrying the girl almost next door offers a minimum of having to face change. But listening to my friends I begin to perceive those forces which would impel an emerging adult to go from the nest and range far afield. Those who have experienced the hidebound traditionalism of the East Coast seem to have been seeking a place where merit and individual worth outweigh what the local social structure dictates. Lack of opportunity and presence of family problems do not seem to be as strong as factors in a leaving. Being known on your own, not as "the son of" seems to be an important factor. In retrospect, my going seems to have been a rebellion against the sameness of what was past and future. Every male in the family worked on the railroad except those still on family farms. A "chicken every Sunday at Grandma's" world of known dimensions. Divorce was unheard of and the words "sex" and "rape" were not used in the local paper. Then why not stay, work there after college days, raise a family along with the girl that maybe I could have married. Perhaps because the things sought, however dimly conceived then in some remote area of the mind, were not to be found there. Or a compelling desire to survive outside of a comfortable niche that could be created there or that already existed. What need to strike out, to become the first college graduate in the family since Mother and Aunt Elsie completed normal school and became teachers in the late 1920's? The first non-railroader. The one who became an army officer, an engineering writer, an attorney. Then ventured to Alaska to a new life in a furtherance of the former quest.

The discussion led we who gather at the church an hour before the Sunday service to lately begin delving into our antecedents in order that we may know more about those we share this time with. Some background beyond the normal sparse amount doled out in social situations, yet not at the level shared by a truly loved spouse or when in the throes of poetic love. Or with an army buddy on the way into combat. This process of looking back leads of course to introspection as to whether much of what has taken place was a going from or a going to - or how much of each. Which process I have been shadow boxing with as I build a new set of social structures in a new place. Shadows of all that has passed before to use as I wish, but without limits as to what I can do. So my thoughts start with the roots that were of English stock moving westward to Kansas as pioneers on the farming side of the family tree. That side had the family farm located in the tri-state mining area in Southeast Kansas and raised eight children, including two sisters who attended what is now Pittsburg State Teachers College before they moved to Kansas City, Kansas. Where one, my mother, a Rickey, married into a family having eight children also, the Chishams, most of whom, and certainly all the males, went to work on the railroad. A post-depression era upbringing in the hot summer and cold winter routine of the middle Mid-West where those before, those in the present, and those after were on a track as to grade school, junior high school, and senior high school. As it was and ever shall be. Boy Scouting, church with mother, brother, and sister every Sunday followed by chicken at Grandma's that involved a nickel streetcar ride over to Rosedale, don't look at the pictures outside the Follies Burlesque Theater on Twelfth Street in Kansas City, Missouri, nothing would ever change. No family car, lots of reading, build radios and model airplanes, camp out on the river down by the Missouri Pacific tracks. Know that the blacks can't come into your neighborhood except to sell ice and to pick up junk - but you are free to cross through their area to get to the river. Some kind of job from age nine on - on December 7, 1941, I was carrying out a neighbor's ashes (stove type), selling magazines, carrying newspapers, doing yard work. Later on to selling ice cream from a three-wheel Cushman motor scooter, and then to working weekends in the mail room at the Kansas City Star. And every high school and college Christmas season, a chance to drag mailbags at the Kansas City Union Station.

A graduation of sort from bicycles to cars of a sort. Which became all-consuming while in high school. A dropping out of the regular church attendance because coming in from work at 5 a.m. Sunday morning was a good excuse. All the while not realizing how much of all that was known would change, was changing, so rapidly.

Out of high school in 1950, with no real goal except that I was expected to go to college someplace with funds that did not exist. Out to Kansas State in Manhattan, Kansas, partly in the belief that it was time to get away from the nest rather than go the junior college route. Journalism seemed to be a good major - who needed to know about business - and something that in a dim way appealed to me. Become adept at finding summer work: carpet wrapper, sugar breaker, floor sweeper and tractor parts order filler, fiberglass worker. Earn the money for the last three years on my own after parents withdrew their limited support when I used some summer money to buy a vintage '39 Chevy. Get the ROTC army commission in Maryland and report for active duty twelve days after graduation in Kansas. Complete the Ordnance Corps Officers Basic Training and ship to Germany for three years. Out in 1957 as Sputnik goes up, meet Senator Jack Kennedy as he campaigns in Topeka, Kansas, and back in the army as there are no openings I can find for an inexperienced journalist in Kansas.

Take the electronic and Nike radar training, write missile reports in New Mexico and the California desert, and after discharge become an engineering writer in the heart of the Atlas weapon system program in San Diego and at remote bases for three years. Find a wife along the way and the 1963 newlyweds become the early

1964 auto accident victims. The injuries lead to a layoff while recovering and a move to Sacramento where new wife has a sister and the economy is better. Except for former engineering writers who can't sell life insurance. At which point a trainee job as an insurance adjuster in Chico, California seems to be what I want to do. Having an expectant wife may have been additional motivation. Chico, for two and one-half years and the birth of two children was a nice place, but did not seem to offer the chance for additional education which I felt a need for. A transfer back to Sacramento allowed use of GI benefits to attend law school at night, to take a better job with Commercial Union Insurance Companies, and to eventually pass the bar, followed by a move back to San Diego to set up a practice in real estate law. After seven years, during a declining real estate market cycle, a failing marriage, and a realization that life is more than working seven days a week, I plan to take the kids I am then raising and head to Alaska where I had thought of moving to years earlier.

The need for a job was met by the offer of one in Upland, California, so my move to Alaska was put off until that work was completed. Two years of bankruptcy related work does not a career make. Now, while working in claims again, for which there seems to be a natural talent, I am seeking the best way to take time to write, to study, to live not apart from the mainstream, but without having too many of the limitations imposed by the need to meet extraordinary needs.

Where does religion fit into all of this? I was raised by a mother who took the kids to church while father worked or stayed home. It was just another part of family life that he did not take part in. Mother would have been a staunch member of whatever denomination she had been exposed to first. We literally left the Methodist Church because their furnace did not work and the United Brethren Church had one that did, even if it meant walking a mile to get there. Mother cut off a good friend who defected to the Catholic Church. Period. Still spoke to the kids but not to the mother. I dropped out of church at the first legitimate chance and over the years saw it a place where people went to be seen rather than to worship. Even after marriage in the highest Episcopal church in San Diego, I did not go, nor did the Episcopal-reared wife until after the children were born. At which time as the result of a parish pastoral visit wherein the associate was late and wine while waiting had impacted on the wife and caused her to agree to help run the Sunday school. After which I attended an inquirer's class and became confirmed. That led to work on the church property in Carmichael, California, and later to much greater involvement at All Souls in San Diego. As a result, even knowing the eternal internal pushing and pulling that goes on in all parishes - like in a family - I find what I need by being a working, active member of a parish family.

And of course this brief overview overlooks so many of the unrecorded things that have been vital to the formative process. The books read, the people encountered, the building blocks of growing up, each causing some nudging in one direction or another. The coming to a point where the road leads in two directions and only one can be taken. In a sense, the times the phone rang but was not answered because of being away at some other chore. And how would things have been different if the message had been received? As counterbalanced by many chance happenings that took place. Be at a time and place to fall in love and a major series of changes and events follow. Or be on the wrong road when the other driver loses control and comes into your lane.

So where and what comes out of all this logging of mileposts, minor and major? Are there any conclusions, if indeed there must be? What factors seen and unseen guided this person to this time and place? Current reading for me for which I am taking time is a biography of Thomas Merton and a collection of Thoreau with emphasis on Walden. There are interesting comparisons and contrasts between the two. It is good input for me at this time. Each set his own course or perhaps had it set for him, yet in a sense seemed predestined for his role or fate. Merton experienced the world but avoided the taking on of secular responsibilities that may have made it less possible to enter into the life of contemplation, study, and writing as a Trappist monk. Thoreau, the walker, observer, teacher who had to help in a family business, but withdrew to Walden to record what he saw and concluded. Neither sought a total withdrawal from mankind and society but rather a situation wherein there was the space and time in which to be able to see and to learn and write of it. Each was successful in the endeavor but at some cost - if such is the losing of material gains from the venture. In a similar mode I have less inclination to study for the Alaska bar examination or to actively seek romantic involvement because each require time devoted, a time and effort commitment that would take time away from those projects presently considered important. All in due course.

Perhaps what I seek is to, in a sense, drop out from part of what urban society expects of its' role players. Not to a life in a converted school bus, not in the sense of the laid-back, looking for an excuse not to work "hippie" - there are enough of that type who are steadily employed. It is more from a feeling that the forty plus years of work have not allowed me the time to learn much that I wish I had. Read the books that I presently know only by title or capsule summary. Take a course in philosophy and one in economics. Build a library of music of all kinds and take time to listen to it. Read back issues of National Geographic. To listen, to see, to be. Not so much a seeking of identity, the often heard battle cry of the departing spouse, as from a realization that there are those things God put here for us to be aware of, not to obscure their presence with that which is created by man: noise, smog, life in the fast lane. And all those creature comforts and "necessities" that camouflage the real world. In the words of Thoreau, "to front only the essential facts of life, and see if I could not learn what it had to teach and not, when I came to die, discover that I had not lived." I know that until the last breath I will be doing, even while sitting, thinking, and viewing. If I am able to meet the standards of duty to self, family, and society, then I will have won. If I neglect self, then I will have lost.

CLEAR AND COLD
FEBRUARY 11, 1985

The clear and cold days that started while I was off to Anchorage last week continue into the new week. Uncle Fats, back after a few days elsewhere, says six degrees as he introduces the marine weather forecast at 6:30 a.m. He is not specific as to whether that is in town or valley. A crucial difference exists as sometimes we are three or four degrees warmer in the Sun Belt area of Juneau. Which would mean that the folks out the road could be down near the zero mark. Before I can find whether his weather comports with my entrance thermometer, I am the recipient of a 6:45 a.m. phone call, which is not an everyday event. In fact, the last one was way back in December when the Christmas crèche was being sent up. And with luck it will be a while before it rings again while I am removing shaving cream from the beard's border. So I learn from an unknown caller that Sister from Fairbanks will be in Juneau at 8:08 a.m. en route to Nicaragua to learn what the problems are there. In spite of the fact that the problems are known and the solution seems to be the real problem. The trip is apparently funded by some concerned citizens of Fairbanks who selected Sister and another lady to go.

So I speed up my slow, don't rush the new week pace, and reroute my thinking toward the airport rather than the office, but forget to call and see if Western really plans to stop in Juneau today. Out the door and there I find that Uncle Fats was right, or at least his report agrees with my thermometer. The Ford fires up immediately even at the low level of warmth, but stops a few times before agreeing to idle. Out to the airport near the Fred Meyer store to see Western Air Lines land an hour later than they are usually scheduled. Looked like a good Juneau landing, but Sister from Fairbanks was not very impressed with the bounce. And immediately wants to know if we are in any danger from the avalanches. She is informed that we confine them to the downtown area where they are more visible. A brief visit, snap a picture, and off she and team member go. Back to town and to work and hope that Tuesday will be less cool. Which it is not.

WILL IT EVER STOP?
FEBRUARY 14-18, 1985

Today, a Thursday, was an eye-opener as to how much snow can come down locally in a short time. A goodly amount fell on Wednesday as the cold spell loosened a bit. No real problem getting the Wagon to move ahead even though the new snow was on top of the four to six inches from Tuesday night. So, after a brief trip downtown at 9 p.m. Wednesday to visit my office and use the plumbing, as the water in the house was still off duty from Wednesday a.m. (No problem at near zero temperatures but warmer weather seems to freeze pipes), I parked as usual far enough off the road to avoid errant snowplows. Thursday morning followed six more inches of snow - or more, as it was far enough up on the car doors to keep them closed until I shoveled a while. After using a dustpan as a scraper/shovel on the windows, I got in, fired up, and prepared to go. But I did not, or rather me and the Wagon did not, as the combination of the new snow and the berm from the previous week, along with ice under the snow, prevented the now desired forward and rearward movement. After digging around the tires and rocking the wagon, a wise decision was made to seek help rather than play further games with a shovel while wearing a suit and tie. After I made a call to the office for help, I spent the waiting time in getting the Wagon ninety degrees from its' original position but no closer to the road. Except that the back bumper was then hanging over the drop-off to the dog house and was in some danger of being in it. The friends with four-wheel drive vehicle arrived and, using the tow rope I had bought in Fairbanks last July for just such an occasion, pulled me the final four feet to the road.

Off to the office and found that the plows had built snowberms down the center of each street so even walking from the parking lot to the office was a new venture. Later, an evening drive to a meeting in the Valley was a way to find that the then falling rain was freezing on the road so it was skate out and back. And watch the funny cars slide as they change lanes.

So the snow continues on a daily basis much as the rain did in January. The twelve inches in twenty-four hours has slowed to perhaps six inches every day. It gives the snowplow people work to do after they are done with the previous batch, plowing and loading and dumping and back for more. The fall did slow enough to allow two trips to the Valley on Saturday; the usual milk run of errands and later attendance at a wedding reception. The Sunday snow allotment was driven along by strong winds, yet it was not cold or unpleasant. And a regular winter wonderland as I smugly watched from my shelter overlooking the channel. Tall trees festooned with snow-covered limbs. Tracks where the rent-a-dogs mushed through on their morning inspection tour. Wind sounds and falling snow sounds. Leading to enjoyment of just setting inside and watching the panorama. Rain late Sunday afternoon washed the tree limbs clean of the snow held by them. But Monday Morn brought a new snow crop and the limbs are again decorated with white.

LENT
FEBRUARY 21, 1985

Suddenly I am awash in rainfall and snowfall and snow melts and in the Lenten season. A chance to see how our all-the-same-but-watch-the-local-rules Anglican Church does it here in Juneau. The basic getting around town and to the Lenten launching is an experience in itself as the state employee parking lot is a chain of lakes in various area as the melted snow and fallen rain of varying depths are locked in by piles of previously plowed snow that is still melting to add to the depths. The busy downtown streets are smaller streams with the sidewalks partly clear and partly covered with ice. An overnight freeze could lead to ice rinks all around us. So Shrove Tuesday (The Day Before Ash Wednesday) came and I was invited to do the guiding of the annual Parish Pancake Supper. A tradition among Episcopalians and others where the cupboards are cleared of fats and flours before the Forty Days. A small amount of promotion led to a surprise turnout and then running out of sourdough batter, ham, juice, and butter. Which led to running out for more supplies. A good evening and good workers such as John Moore, Dwight Broga, Jim Griffith, Don Hitchcock, Fr. Dale

Sarles, and many others including J.B., age 12, who was also a good consumer of the product. Also a chance to introduce Dutch Babies to Holy Trinity and thereby bring a bit of the past from All Souls in San Diego and to remember those past Shrove Tuesdays over the years. Then on to Ash Wednesday and the 5 p.m. service with the imposition of ashes and the very solemn start of the time wherein self-examination and doing without lead up to the Easter Sorrow and Glory. Thursday started the opportunity to attend daily Morning Prayer which I arrive at after it is over. The clock will just have to be reversed thirty minutes in the a.m. so that I can partake of this early service. I did manage to get to the first of the series of Lenten Lunches which was attended by about ninety people who had soup, homemade bread and a rousing "Faith In Action" talk by the Roman Bishop, Father Kennedy. Our parish hall was filled to overflowing; having a stage set up for a small theater group did not make it any bigger. So on into the Holy Season Of Lent, in the new setting which really is like the old in many ways.

SATURDAY
FEBRUARY 23, 1985

Now that I have passed the six-month mark in my Juneau tenure, it would appear that an answer is possible to the question about what a person, single or otherwise, does in Juneau on a Saturday when there are no fish to catch or deer to chase. The obvious answer is that the day is spent very much like anyplace else. Except that here one starts out in rain and very likely later encounters snow. And if the errands were not done during the week due to work or other limiting circumstances, it is when they are listed and hopefully done. Such as: Have a leisurely breakfast and two large cups of coffee while looking for the things to take along. Like the claim check to get the coat out of the cleaner shop, the film to be left somewhere, the coupon so that the film processing will cost less, a prescription, and the list of "things" to do. Out to the Valley even though some of the "things" are in "Town" and all could be done there except for the Auke Bay mail getting. Find the pharmacy at Nugget Rexall and leave the prescription for filling. Somehow, when the dentist gives the pain relief order three weeks before the work, I feel uneasy. Look for a new pair of gloves while waiting, but none are on sale. Get the pills and then make an unscheduled stop at Hearthside Book Store where I find a copy of Thoreau Collected at a good price and I need one so that the public library can have their copy back. Buy a raffle ticket from a nurse's group. The prize is a trip for two to Palm Springs, California or other warm spot costing the same air fare. Nurse not included. Down the mall to Nugget Department Store to see if Daughter gets a new coat but no sales on. Later. Stop in at Alaska Air Lines to say hello to Kathy Parker, one of the nicest people in our singles group. Their supersaver fares don't start till after Western's so can't switch the planned trip Outside to Alaska Airlines. Then browse in the Gourmet Accent place of fine cooking things - where I buy a veal smasher and a garlic basket, both indulgences which I do not totally need. Greet two friends who are breakfasting at a café. Cross the road to the bank in the Jordan Creek Mall where the check for teaching the cooking class is exchanged for cash. Which stop was after Jerry's Meat Market where prices are studied in case of need to do future business there. On to the Airport Center to retrieve the coat which had a button sewn on to a backing button in a way that I could not do. Out to Auke Bay for mail and to harass the clerk about the two-cent postal rate increase. Then back down the road toward town and the mandatory stop at Fred Meyer where a coat for Daughter is the first objective. Or a search for one. During which, as could be expected, a lady of my acquaintance comes by and inquires as to whether I am finding one that I like. At least this time I am not buying shoes with high heels. Give up on imagining how long the arms would have to be and look for tire chains instead. For the car. Nowadays they come in a nice blue plastic case which allows off-season storage. Which is a long way from the good old days of a wet potato sack. The Fifty Dollar price is also quite distant from the last set that I bought. Another purchase delayed as I don't need them Fifty Dollars worth. I may regret the decision later. I also don't buy the spray stuff that is supposed to be used in place of chains. It goes on the tire and the ice in front of the tire. After a brief pause, just drive on. Or so it says. The real secret may be that the wait causes the driver to calm down and be able to ease out of the difficulty. So, on to the Baranoff Bookstore where a book is being held for addition to my reading list. Then home to dump the stuff off and then out to look at lots where I might live in a cabin existence. The vacant one is up a hill past a house and the Ford declines to dominate the icy slope. So I back out and go on to a cabin that needs some work. It is nicely located as I see from the road and decide not to wade across the creek and over the snowbanks to see it up close. The now-falling snow has caused me to put off the viewing. Home again to meet with the dishes in the sink. Then off to a grand tour of Foodland and replacement of certain food items consumed during the past week. Which winds up the day, except for a benefit dinner to help the International Christian Youth Exchange. The program involves hors d'oeuvres at one place, dinner and program at a second, and dessert at a third. By now I wonder if the Ford is tiring of all the starts and stops. At least tomorrow will be a light day with only the pre-church discussion group, church with choir duty plus lesson reading and chalice bearing, coffee hour, a possible brunch with the singles group, laundry, housecleaning, and reading and writing projects. Another QUIET weekend.

REFLECTIONS AT THE SIX-MONTH MARK
FEBRUARY 25, 1985

Just after 11 p.m. on a Monday night, with the sound of rain falling outside the windows of my bedroom/study/writing place. I have had the light turned out for a while and my rotating reading chair turned so that I can look at the city lights and their reflections on the waters of Gastineau Channel. As accompanied by the distant sounds of traffic on Egan Drive on the other side of the channel and the lights of occasional cars on the bridge over to here on Douglas Island. Reflections also of an inward nature as I think of the six months that have passed since that August night - also rainy - when I arrived here. How have things worked out, is it what I expected, what have I done or left undone since coming here?

For the most part, life here is very much what I expected, similar in most ways to life anywhere else but with just enough differences to make it unique. The weather is not as cold as I was considering when Fairbanks seemed to be the place where I would be. And less of the unofficial state bird, the mosquito, in residence here. Work is a five-day week doing a job I enjoy with compatible people. Outside of work, there are enough things going on locally that one does not lack for activities. The writing projects, church, and other things that I do leave little time to be concerned with cabin fever. Once again, a short time in a new place and more than enough to do. Which may be the only negative reflection. I don't have the time so far to do the things we Alaskans, new or not, are by myth supposed to be doing. And some of which I am not ready for anyway. Such as the bear, squaw, and bottle test. Or sleeping in the open at minus seventy degrees on the Brooks Range. The job and the winter so far have kept me from extensive and successful fishing and deer hunting. Hiking is a venture that waits as is cross-country skiing. I have been able to fill the role of an Urban Sourdough coming into the wet and cool country and enjoyed the place and the people. The next step is to get out and away and learn to know the rest of the state.

The major benefit, personally, in addition to a steady income, is a lower stress level even when I consider the waiting list of projects. You do what you can and don't worry about the rest. And the days when the rain slows for a few hours always opens new vistas to gaze toward. I also like being near the water again, a comfort I much enjoyed in the San Diego days. Juneau is a friendly, open place with some small townishness, but not too much. There is a spirit of community that was lacking in many other places I have been. Perhaps part of the acceptance, aside from being in a place chosen by God to display his splendor, is changes within. Seventeen or eighteen years ago when living in a smaller town in California, the urge was to get to a place where educational opportunities were greater and where life moved a little faster. Now I appreciate more the pace of a place like this which is a good blend of quality elements for a good life. And yet no feeling of being confined to an island even though it is a long flight or boat ride out. When one wants to go outside. We don't have next door major league sports so have to resort to cable TV, which is how most of us would see them anyway. And there is intellectual stimulation here to the particular extent desired. Not to mention having more degrees per capita then almost anywhere. It is also much easier to find and fit into a group such as singles, writers, artists, cooks, than any place I have ever lived. And as the greatest enticement, we have so far avoided the greatest scourge of our civilization, fast food places all over the landscape. Which may not last but is nice not to have for a while.

AT WORK
FEBRUARY 27, 1985

A Wednesday. One of those days at the office when the phone is somewhat undemanding and the mid-week mail is light. Adequate time to read a file that originated four and one-half years ago and is still not near a resolution. At least it provides a nice history of people who have worked in my job, attorneys who have contributed to the mass of papers in the file along with doctors who have provided reams of non-conclusive medical information, and the words of various witnesses. Four hours of reading and review lead me to the conclusion that there is no solution except to pay lots of money. From little accidents great expenses grow. The day, prior to the file reading, started with a Lenten time Morning Prayer service at the Church, followed by picking up (my turn) of "sticky buns" for the office and trying to juggle the goodies, the briefcase, and a stockpot of soup out of the wagon and over the melting ice and snow and into the S.O.B. where the elevators were on the daily slow cycle causing a shortness of temper as I waited. Then, to go up, one must ride the elevator down before going up or not be able to get on when it stops again at the ground level.

The cables to the non-operational adjacent elevator can of course be seen in the lobby of the lower level. The highlight of the day for we Fifth Level window users was watching a local attorney find a parking ticket on his car in the city lot across the street. And seeing how deftly he placed the ticket on another car in the same lot. He does not know that one of us descended to the lot level and retrieved the ticket from the other car. Fun time will be when the attorney does not appear in court. He may have some explaining to do as the meter maid was advised by police radio of the ticket switch and may have flagged the master copy. And a quiet afternoon after the ticket caper. Except for a call from Sister From Fairbanks who is actually calling from somewhere in the Lower Forty-Eight. Which led me to drive out to the airport near the Fred Meyer Store after dinner to see her for five minutes before she reboarded Western on the last leg of her journey back from Nicaragua. The observation tour apparently confirmed what has been reported on about the conditions there below the Lower Forty-Eight and raises ongoing questions as why we are involved there. On the road again and back to home and fire while wondering why I can't seem to get more concerned about banana wars that have gone on as long as I can remember.

SUNDAY, SUNNY AGAIN
MARCH 3, 1985

Into March 1985, with no March Ides yet appearing. Only a weekend that started with wet, blowing snow and then presented us with sunshine most of Sunday. This was Taku Rondy weekend in Juneau, our local effort to break out of any lingering cabin fever that might exist and to celebrate eventual spring. Which is when we have spring rains rather than winter, fall, or summer rains. There is a difference, I am told. The Rondy (short for ron-d-voo) will continue on this week. I did not manage to attend the kickoff event Friday evening which was the Boy Scout fund raising that was a celebrity pie-in-the-face-for-a-fee. Targets were some better known local faces such as Uncle Fats, the politicians who normally have egg on their faces anyway, and the head of the school board. My plan was to wear my Rondy pin to avoid any lockup and to later watch the tug-of-war (not the one going on in the legislative session) and perhaps the Rondy-related Great Boat Show. The Chile Feed and the Lions Club Pancake Breakfast sounded interesting but more food I can do without. So I hurried my Saturday Valley rounds going from mall to mall (if they had carpet between them, would it be mall to mall carpet?) and checked in at Fred Meyer to watch the people trying to hit each other in the parking lot. Also took time to stop at a sale of used restaurant equipment to see if by chance they had a stockpot of commercial dimensions, perhaps a used cleaver and maybe a cutting board. No on all three items. Now I have two heavy duty spatulas, a large ceramic bowl which should hold fourteen quarts of anything that I serve, a small scoop for scooping, a wire whip to use for anything that my four other wire whips can't do, and the most needed, long-sought treasure: a pancake batter dispenser for only $15.00. Now, at the annual Shrove Tuesday Pancake Supper, a setting of the selector knob will cause batter for pancakes of various diameters to be placed precisely on the grill. What a find! Not too practical for the average Sunday at home so maybe I can store garlic in it. With my finds, I was off to Front Street by 2 p.m. to watch the tug-of-war, where I found several other fans and some familiar faces in the fair-sized crowd. The center of Front Street was occupied by a two-inch manila rope about two hundred feet long. Members of several teams were ready to challenge the bunch from the Red Dog Saloon, a well known local business place on Front Street. That team seemed to have had the most practice in the art of stomach expansion and outweighed the next beefiest group by some one thousand pounds. Which, on a ten-man team, is no small feat. Each team had an anchor person of generous girth who was looped with the end of the rope. As the Red Dog team seemed to be immovable in any direction they did not want to go, they dominated the men's division. Even the highly rated team from the Triangle Club was able to hold them for only a few seconds. The Juneau Empire ladies' team won their first match and were celebrating the final match prematurely when the opposition team pulled them over the line. A fun time as the rain fell. On to Foodland and home. From where I take time to follow the rent-a-dog tracks in the snow toward the channel. It is apparently easier for them than me as there are several down slopes to negotiate. Not a path for traveling in darkness. The rewards of walking on the rocky beach and seeing the hull hulks of several abandoned fishing boats made the walk worthwhile. Now I know for sure that I can fish this summer from near my doorstep. Catching the fish may be something else, but it is the fishing and not necessarily the catching that makes the past-time enjoyable. Then today was the boat show and the display of the tempting toys of summer. Prudence prevailed somehow and it will still be the $49.50 boat this summer. If a motor is found in time. At that price, motor not included. And with the sun still shining, on to visit the Laundromat and to see if the one dryer is still unrepaired for six weeks in a row. We regulars notice those critical details. While the washer toiled, off on a drive to take pictures of the snow on the mountains that surround us. A rare chance to record blue sky and the mountains before fog, snow, rain, or some other form of meteorological event interfered. Where else can one emerge from a supermarket, Laundromat, church, or bank and be witness to such scenery? The finale for Sunday was an hour at the Perseverance Theater watching performances of one-act plays by New Directions, a local showcase-training ground for starting play writers, actors, and directors. Nicely done and perhaps a place where my in-process play efforts can be submitted when done. On to Monday again.

THE LEGISLATIVE PROCESS

MARCH 8, 1985

Thursday of a busy week, which started with two days of sunshine and cold before getting back to the usual business of rain and snow competing for attention. Which said six inches of snow overnight left a nice berm to be jumped with Ford onto the road this morning. After a noontime Lenten Lunch Series with our Director as the speaker, I was routed off to a new part of my work. Which was to attend a hearing on proposed legislation seeking to change a part of the workers compensation laws of the state. My first official visit to the interior of the State Capitol which is located outside the back (upper) Main Street entrance of the S.O.B. My work time duties include keeping up on new laws and what may become new laws. So I entered the Capitol and found my way to Room 102 which is where 202 would be if the second floor was not the first floor. This may result from the steep terrain locally and a tendency to have a ground floor below a first floor level in many of the public buildings. Except as in the S.O.B. where we enter off Willoughby at Level 2 and then can descend to Level 1 which leads to a lower parking level. To further compound the confusion, the Upper Main Street entrance is either up a flight of stairs carved out of the rock near where the old jail was before the S.O.B., which leads to entry at Level 8 or at Level 7 if a walk is followed to the loading dock area. Unless one enters through the A.O.B. (Administrative Office Building) off Main Street and goes to the third level thereof to cross over a walkway and emerge onto Level 8 of the S.O.B.

The immediate impression on entering the Capitol is that in contrast to the low pace of the S.O.B., things were humming along in the legislative hallways. People were moving a bit faster and all seemed to have urgent business at hand. As the hearing I was to hear was preceded by one on real estate time-sharing laws, I waited in the hall outside of the office of Representative Navarre where the hearings were to be held. Which gave me a chance to observe the aides, pages, and legislators in action, probably in the same mold as other states except for a bit more casual dress here. Lots of papers being handed back and forth, messages conveyed, and just plain politicking. Such as the arm over the adjacent shoulder maneuver while walking and talking down the hall. Also the conferring face-to-face in great and intense seriousness before a spin-off to the next objective. Very impressive and a sense of THINGS BEING DONE! When I finally found a seat in the hearing room, I had my first introduction to tele-conferencing, wherein testimony for or against the bill under scrutiny was to be taken from various people throughout the state. Pro and con comments heard from Soldotna and Anchorage and other places before the time for the hearing ran out and it was put over again to another day. So back to the S.O.B. and the world away from the power brokers.

FOR SALE
MARCH 14, 1985

On my way back from the governor's office this morning, where I was taking a TELEX message that somehow came into our office instead of his (perhaps he does not have a machine there: ours rings once or twice a day and types out some urgent words from afar), I noted one of the unique things about our town. I have lived in other cities where the Supermarkets and Laundromats provide bulletin boards for the local citizens to post cards listing items for sale and services offered. These sometimes typed, sometimes handwritten indicia of what one person has and another might want or even actually need are usually on a three by five card drafted with the intent to reveal what is offered along with a telephone number or even an address to use in finding out more details. Or to make an offer. Now I realize with amazement as I walk past the board on the eighth floor of the S.O.B. that Juneau has raised the bulletin board art form to a pristine level unequaled in other venues. None of the "sitter available", "lost dog", "sofa for sale" small lettered listings of the type favored in the Lower 48: here there are full page flyers, photographs in living color attached to some, to enhance very artistic descriptions of real property, boats, cars, freezers, and fish smokers. These add a feeling of really shopping for what you need while on the normal rounds during the day. When I find myself in need of some household item - or even when I don't, I check the eighth floor, the Court Building Lobby, Foodland's entrance, and the ones in the Nugget Mall as a matter of routine. There might just be some deal too good to pass up. Even listings for house sharing are posted as "Non-smoking, Christian, petless, quiet person sought to share deluxe two bedroom on bus line." Those seem to stay up the longest. Lately I have been looking for a bed for the spare room and a motor for my boat, the motor being needed if I ever get the bottom of the boat watertight. Beds are in short supply lately so I watch the boards more often. Today there was a listing of a queen-sized mattress, tired but clean, which might be a good interim measure till a better one is found. And it is free. But no answer at the number. On Tuesday I did see a deal on a boat motor and must follow-up. "$400. OBO, 25 Horse Johnson, only in saltwater four times." I hope that one of those was not under said saltwater for an extended time. The only limitation on this method of seeking what you need is that the same cards are posted on many boards, causing duplication of effort for the seeker. Not to mention the poster. The use of home telephone numbers when most of the people are at work, finding the tags with the telephone number all torn off, and trying to get through the 8 ½ by 11 car and house spectaculars to find what you really want are also minor irritations. Most of the boards are purged on a regular basis to allow a fresh batch of offerings; the photos go if not claimed by the purge day. The total concept is like a perpetual garage sale where something is found and a call is made rather than trying to find a remote spot on Back Loop Road or at the top of a snowy driveway. There is also the protection of being an unknown voice on the phone with less pressure to buy than when you realize you know the seller. There is also a protocol used when posting a notice or taking down a number. Most posters prefer to remain anonymous and wait till viewers have moved on - or with assertiveness move other notices so that their listing is in an uncluttered area. Those finding a treasure take a nonchalant air so as to not disclose their find, and memorize the number for future use. Only the bold take a tag or write openly. These are the folks who also are willing to admit that they use toothpicks in public.

SPRING ARRIVES
MARCH 20, 1985

Vernal Equinox time as what is springing forth out on North Douglas Road is light snow to go with the windshield ice which has resulted from the rain of the previous evening. The day starts as the well went dry Tuesday night, again, and the 1,500 gallon reserve tank for the two houses is empty. An unusual lack of rain over the past two days has caused the rainwater supplemental system to not work and thereby the water problem is compounded. So I heat water from the supply of gallon jugs that are now kept on hand and take a quasi bath while standing in the tub and dipping water from my largest mixing pan - the one that I use for salad for fifty. It will have to scrubbed before the next fifty arrive. Then, reasonably clean, off to town in the wagon with the sour transmission. Stop for the sticky buns for the office as a result of a lost wager on one case at law. Then, before work, find a parking spot where an exit without reverse gear is possible and, after leaving buns and briefcase at the office, on by foot to the Morning Prayer service as a Lenten task. Somehow, perspective is necessary in order to accept that we had our spring on Monday and Tuesday of this week, that if the $850. a month apartment has water on twenty-eight out of thirty days, it is a good month, especially if it is February, and that one can drive a long way in low range if the alternative is to make some mechanic's day complete. At least the stars were out in full view when I went out to thump the water tank to see if it was indeed empty. Even when I had my dental-type stitches out at noon, it was nice to have the dentist and his staff comment favorably on my latest letter to the editor of our local paper. Late afternoon of this first spring day brings snowflakes in a swirl; they average one inch in size. I know this to be true because so many land and lie on the ledge outside of the office window, a pause before they become a spot of dampness. Others are sturdy enough to bounce off of the adjacent wall and descend toward Willoughby Street where their fate is met on the sidewalk and pavement. Within minutes the size of the flakes diminishes a bit and then increases to the previous splendor. Before end-of-work time the whole scene is back to clear and windy with the snow off somewhere else entertaining other Juneauites. Thursday is a bit more spring-like even though the level of relative warmth or coolness is just under freezing early in the day. It turns out to be a walking-type day as, after parking, I leave a dish for lunch at the office and again make the walk to the Church and back. That involves climbing the stairs to level five, the first stop, then stairs to level seven, and out the back of the

S.O.B. before the four blocks to the church by 7:30 a.m.. Back down from level seven to level five when I return. Later, down to level two and over to the Convention Center for an hour of seminar on halibut fishing as part of the lecture series that the Forest Service sponsors. An hour away from work that I will make up in the evening. At noon, back to level five and follow the route to the Church for the Lenten Lunch and speaker and back to work on the reverse path. The high point of the luncheon was seeking the recipe for the soup and finding among the ladies in the kitchen one of indeterminate years named Liz who prepared the soup. One of those whom we should never denigrate by calling them senior citizens: rather they should be considered a national treasure because of what they have in the way of wisdom and experience that we could all benefit from. My last walking trip was to be to drop off church news items at the Empire; that I decided to save until Friday. And the meeting of the singles group in the Valley in the evening didn't involve walking as the low range only car made the run out and back in its' usual stolid manner. On to Friday when, as I leave for work, the water system takes another day off. At least the dishes are done and the weekend is in sight. This might be the ideal time to use the shower at the Laundromat - except how does one get the dryer to work from inside after taking the shower? However that goes, Monday is Seward's Day and we Alaskans will be off in honor of he who was wise enough to buy this real estate in 1867.

MR. SEWARD'S DAY
MARCH 25, 1985

Seward's Day, 1985, which for those of us Alaskans employed by the State of Alaska is a holiday to honor Mr. Seward, who engineered the purchase of this real estate from the Russians several years ago. The sum that he convinced the Federal Treasurer to pay for all this vastness would not now go very far toward a day of present Federal expense. It turned out to be a good deal in spite of what the nay sayers thought at the time the escrow closed. So Mr. Seward is every year honored throughout the state. Although for some at the time he was not so well regarded in one village where he visited after the purchase and did not respond properly to the local customs, which caused him to become carved facing the wrong way on a local totem pole. I appreciate what he did anyway as it gives me an opportunity to practice taking time off past the weekend. To the extent of staying up late Sunday to watch a mediocre movie on the TV and to sleep in till 7 a.m., at which time I noticed that the pines outside the window were not the green hue they had been at sundown. All were now laden with white. After finding my spectacles, I was able to see that the path I had followed from the beach late Sunday was now under six inches of new snow with more being deposited. Further confirmation came by radio as Uncle Fats intoned that the buses would not be trying to get up Cordova Street and that there would be afternoon sunshine. So up the stairs to consider coffee and a breakfast more than the diet of the workday but less than the gluttony of the weekend. No wantonness of the weekend with bacon and eggs and hot cakes stacked high. With the eggs fried in the bacon grease as sort of a gesture toward the doctors who discourage such things. Have to live just a bit. So I settle for a double portion of cream-of-wheat over butter and with brown sugar but use low fat milk to keep it lo-cal. An egg fried in butter is used to enhance the English muffin which was buttered before going back under the broiler to melt the cheese on top of the butter. Even the water going off again as I chortle over the fixings does not deter me. The food is enjoyed without the accompaniment of the TV news; the scene out back of the falling snow is too pleasant to be sullied by noise. A second cup of coffee as I browse the remains of the Anchorage Sunday paper, which I had ignored on Sunday. The sun does appear later and the slow pace continues as I read of fishing, do the dishes when the water comes on and catch up on catching up. A good day.

PALM SUNDAY
MARCH 31, 1985

Another Lenten Season builds closer to the depths and heights of Holy Week as Palm Sunday is celebrated in my new church community. Our Alaska Bishop is in town as the Town and Valley groups join in one worship celebration in the borrowed facilities at Floyd Dryden Middle School. A middle school is one where the kids get grades six, seven, and eight so that they can then proceed to a four-year high school rather than attending seven-eight-nine before ten, eleven, and twelve. It must make sense to the school board. Our valley church presence results from the population shifting that way while there is still a need for the historic church in town to fill a role there. The Palm Sunday Service is the first that I have ever attended where, due to physical limitations and perhaps because of the rain outside, the processional of clergy, choir, and attendees to the strains of "All Glory, Laud, and Honor" is omitted. In years past as All Souls, San Diego, palm fronds were dispensed in the Parish Hall prior to the journey along Catalina Boulevard to the church proper in a joyous march. Then for two years in a row at St. Marks in Upland, California, the procession was led into the church by a child on horseback and down the main aisle to the altar area. The horse was named Jinks and was provided by my employer and his daughter which was their annual connection with things churchy. The first year Jinks made the journey revealed a "non-empty" horse status which existed until just prior to the procession which caused the choir to step lively and the ushers to rush for appropriate implements. Here, in my new church home, I am learning that like many things here, we make do for a place or a solution. Which is why a school library is as good a place as any to worship. After the service, I note that many of the books on the library shelves differ in content from the ones of my era. Paul Bunyan and Penrod may be there somewhere but the trend seems to be otherwise. "Drug Smuggling - The International Connection" competes with volumes on the role of women in society, life in the divorced family, and introduction to sexuality as the subject mater. All are adventures stories of a sort but not the sort that I read in the days of yore.

MAUNDY THURSDAY
APRIL 4, 1985

Our spring continues to grow in stature with full daylight by 6 a.m. This makes it easier for those of us up at that time, willingly or not, to preview the conditions outside the windows. Not that the sound of rain daily isn't a fairly good indicator by itself. Except for a few hours of heavy snow and a minimal amount of teasing sunshine, there has been rain day and night for most of the week. While it does mean less snow at our level, Eaglecrest Ski Area has been trying to uncover the top of the lift where some two hundred inches of snow is in residence. We are at that time of the year when the long days may necessitate pulling curtains closed if sleeping late is desired. And where it is not yet realistic to leave for work without proper footwear to conquer the vagaries of the day. A decision to wear "low quarter" shoes without protective coverings could mean water damage from snow or wading. So I opt for the desert boots, relics of California days. They are not good on ice or snow but less likely to be damaged by snow or water. Along with the rain, I am enjoying another sign of spring. The boats on the channel are increasing in number as the fishing season nears. Now I know for sure that I have survived a winter in Alaska. So on Friday I take the big gamble and try on city shoes. They seem initially awkward after months of boots but with practice are tolerated for a day and again on Saturday at the Easter Vigil as Lent ends. Last Saturday was pre-Palm Sunday as I was locked in an encounter with eight pounds of beans being converted to bean soup for Tuesday's dinner at the Glory Hole. This Saturday is get-ready-for-Easter Sunday time which is why I was carrying two watermelons out of the S.O.B. on Thursday. A leaving directed by our Senior Warden - Division Director so that I could decorate the exterior and stuff the interior with a fruit compote of sorts. At least the melons won't take as much space in the reefer as the five gallons of bean soup. Which melon project along with scrambled eggs for ninety at Easter Breakfast (18.5 dozen eggs to go with ham and festive breads) keep me on the go till time for the Festal Eucharist choir duties. Even with all the fellowship of this blessed season, I still feel a tinge of nostalgia for the past celebrations of this Holy Time at the church in San Diego. So I later take a walk on the beach with the rent-a-dogs, look north toward those mountains and east to Mt. Juneau and down the channel and know that this is now home.

SPRING TIME IN ALASKA
APRIL 13-14, 1985

According to those who were here when we later arrivers got here, a "sourdough" is one who has lived through a winter in Alaska. Those fable sayers can also quote several other definitions of the term, such as sour on Alaska and no dough to get anywhere else. Anyone living here who is not a sourdough is a cheechako till the end of the first winter. That roughly translates into what in the Lower 48 would be called a tenderfoot. Having now become an official sourdough, I wonder if I will be able to survive the spring. It is not the temperature; that stays near freezing at night and can escalate up past forty degrees during the day. It is not the rain; that is here regardless of the season. Death, Taxes, and Rain are the certainties here. Even the occasional winds sweeping up the channel are not hard to accept, nor is the snow. What is most difficult to accept is that any and all of the above can come on in rapid succession, separately, jointly, or in any combination. Such as on the weekend. Saturday morning was clear and spring-like as I ventured out without hat or gloves for a Valley meeting. During the meeting snow began to fall in copious amounts but did not pile up. Then the rains came. After a clear spell, the cycle started again. The evening brought pellets of coarse snow. Sunday morning was bright with sunshine till after church, when snow started to fall along with the rising wind. The day ended with no rain or snow, just overcast. Till 2 p.m. Sunday, the weather was background for another busy time. Saturday was time to plan, over breakfast, the Single's May program and events. Then to the bookstore to pick up a special-order book before the weekly visit to Foodland. This was followed by a few hours in the kitchen prepping for two potlucks. No one really takes potluck to a potluck; everything is carefully planned. No one takes leftovers. The quiche for Sunday's post-service farewell to our retired bishop - interim rector was the first try at a new recipe. Like all quiches, this one was not done in the stated time. They never are. The thirty-to-forty minutes cook time was one hour and still counting. Even the dish for the Saturday evening potluck was started and finished in that time. Neither dish generated me any leftovers. After the second potluck I retire to home to watch what happens outside: snow, rain or whatever. The season has one foot in winter and one in spring. Sunshine at work time and rain at playtime. And never complacent.

NOW IT'S SPRING
APRIL 21, 1985

Sunday seems to be the first demonstration where Juneau has tried to show that a sunny beautiful day can last all day without rain. The erratic weather of springtime gave way on Saturday to a few hours of stability before today's glory. After weeks of wind and rain amid a few clear periods, some being as long as three hours, there came a usable weekend. Saturday's sunshine was not diminished in the least by light rain from time to time which, with the temperature rising to over forty degrees, created a near tropical setting.

Being without wheeled transportation as the Wagon is in for repairs while the dealer tries to sell me something new, I spent the day on a volunteer project for American Youth Hostel. The local group is renovating a downtown home for the use of their touring members. One of the AYH local leaders picked me up as the weight of my toolbox is too great for me to tote to town on foot. The leader's VW Squareback predates even my Ford. The house under renovation is at Sixth and Harris above downtown and was built and owned by the Whiteheads, a Juneau family of long residency. The goal of the present work is to convert the house into facilities to house up to forty AYH travelers plus house-parents. It is large enough to do so gracefully even if it is not as big as the Guv's place which is higher up the hill. With four bedrooms, three fireplaces, multiple bathrooms, and a basement that has more square footage than most homes have all together, it is a mammoth project. My contribution was to remove an interior wall of double thick plaster, scrape linoleum paste off the kitchen floor, and dig a hole for a fire exit outside of a basement window. That gave time to rest on the shovel occasionally and look around a part of Juneau that I have not visited before. It is up from the Church and borders an area of homes that cling to the edge of the steep slope just below the trees that march to the top of the slopes. This was original Juneau before the first large scale move out Glacier Highway and the later Valley sprawl. A glorious day during which the muscles of winter demonstrate their need for springtime attention. And that one was followed by Sunday, Monday, and Tuesday with the sun, warmth, and the increasing parade of boats on the channel. Time to walk to work and enjoy the view from the bridge up and down the channel. And to welcome a few minutes of fragrant rain late Tuesday.

THE OFFER
APRIL 24, 1985

Since arriving in Alaska, one of my prior much enjoyed pastimes has been given greater opportunity for development. This is the sometimes neglected art of writing to family and close friends when the writing urge overtakes me. Some of the recipients even write back; a few with more regularity than others. One has promised to call before sending a letter as the shock of a reply might damage my health. As might a reply or any letter from the children who are away at schools. There is, however, one newly acquired pen pal who promises never to forget me. Every week seems to bring a new greeting from this one. The start of this now one-sided correspondence was when I saw an advertisement in a national magazine and accepted an opportunity to buy a workable fishing reel for only $4.00. Any reel that functions at all would seem to be worth that nominal sum. So, thinking of friends and small children, I not only ordered one for me but went for the five allowed to early purchasers who sent along the original of the magazine ad. That gave me the added bonus of the reel being loaded with six pound test line. What a deal! Before I could get the order in the mail, I saw that the same company was offering a home tool kit of forty-five pieces for only $5.00 plus postage. Why not order five of those; they come in a fitted case and are guaranteed for a full five years. The perfect gift for tool-less friends. A second order was conceived. Eight weeks later the reels arrived in all their glory complete with sticky paper decal decorative stripes to be stuck onto each reel. They do work; the bearing noise will certainly alert the user to when the reel is turning. And the stripe offsets the pot metal construction. So far I have managed to leave one on a doorstep but have had no takers for the others. The tools arrived shortly after the reels. Not a bad deal even if top-heavy with small screwdrivers of every persuasion. The hammer and the pliers can both be hidden in my hand - at the same time. The set is useful for occasional (read extreme emergency) use or is useful as a guide in buying what is really useful. I had barely opened the tool delivery when I received the watch offer; the one with the calculator that will do your taxes for you. Goodbye, CPA. I was one of a select million to be given this chance to buy. Which I declined. That did not stop the company from offering me the chance to, using a $23.00 discount coupon, buy the Chef Bornshaft Knife Set for $3.95. I was still looking at the picture of the chef and the knives that will balance on the edge of a razor when I was advised that I had won the prize in a new promotion. Full circle! I get

$25,000. Or a one caret Black Star of India, whatever that is. No purchase necessary but if I would like to buy a special reel........It is nice to know that somewhere in New Jersey is a company that thinks of me so often. Who could ever be lonely with a pen pal like that? The fact that they apparently sold one million reels that appear to cost much less than one dollar to make does not make me feel unkindly toward them. After all, someone has to try to keep the workers in Taiwan and Hong Kong busy turning out reels, knives, and calculators. And where would Chef Bornshaft be, not to mention the printers of all the literature?

MAY DAY
MAY 1, 1985

A new month, a new page on the desk calendar as I do away with the notes, coffee splash artwork, and doughnut tracings of April. Morning and month started with near-rain as I got the month underway by heading south on North Douglas toward the bridge. Walking to work most days results from the Wagon not being ready to move without a transmission and the possible new car being five weeks from delivery. The exercise of a twenty minute walk, mandatory or not, becomes the fitness program that was to start on New Year's Day. The bus that comes in from North Douglas at 7:30 a.m. or the co-employees who come in a little before that time could be used instead of foot work, but for now I prefer the 120 steps per minute up and down. In so doing, I learn again that shoes, socks, and feet must be matched firmly. Also that city shoes are either carried or left at the office for daytime use. And that a minimum of briefcase baggage is in order. Rain hats are to be firmly affixed or bound down with the parka hood while on the Douglas Bridge. The penalty is to watch loose headgear descend to the channel below. The apex of the bridge slope is the place for the mandatory look south toward Taku Inlet and north toward the Valley from whence cometh the streams of commuter traffic. Then off to the city side of the bridge, cross Egan Drive and head south past the Parkshore condo complex, admire Foodland from the unkempt rear areas, cross Gold Creek - no salmon yet- and past the Prospector where the breakfasters are watching cars, walkers, and the channel. Cross the parking lot to the S.O.B. and think of the summer hikes of longer duration that this will prepare me for. There is a definite advantage to walking as long as a car is available for errands and groceries: time to think, to watch the emerging Juneau tulips, to see how much trash was missed on the cleanup effort of last Saturday, to realize that it is possible to exist without full time use of a car. Until the snow starts to fall anyway when I may rethink about confronting snow and darkness.

Otherwise this has been the week of HB 318, the lost cat, and the house. HB 318 is a piece of proposed legislation intended to help injured workers get back to their former jobs. As it involves worker's compensation and rehab efforts and therefore Risk Management, which is our division's task, the proposal is favored. The House Committee considering the bill invites comment and support (hopefully) by teleconference. I walk to the Capitol and wait to voice my support - three times waiting and three times that the matter is put over to another time. An aside comment regarding some awkward words in the bill results in a full scale airing of who said what and shows whose ego was bruised by not getting credit for a sensible change. After all the flack and the trips, the last changes are made and my words in support are never heard. Next year, the same bill may show up again as this session is down to thirteen days and the state budget is still being pursued. This is the biggie to be acted on or it will be into the ten-day overrun after which everyone finally goes home.

And on Sunday the cat that I got on Saturday got out. Having been gifted with cat (gray tabby with gold trim, spayed, housebroken) plus cat bed and toys, I invested in cat box, cat box filler, and found the year old cat food imported from California. A cat was needed as the one left in the Lower 48 for later arrival is now too old to travel. And I could do a favor to the family dog of a family that accepted two cats to replace the one that had gone to the Great Sandbox In The Sky. Which two cats nearly caused trauma with the family dog who retreated outside to pout. My new resident adapted quickly to the latest home and even enjoyed the unfinished room and bath on the lower level where it followed me on Sunday. Apparently the cat found where the shower drain will be, an opening that I was unaware of. Somewhere on North Douglas is a house cat looking for a home. I would go on a house-to-house search except that the houses are far apart and I would feel funny asking if a cat had showed up that responds to being whistled for. And if it comes back this weekend, I will be away to Fairbanks closing the deal on the house there as, now being enamored of Juneau, such a possession is no longer necessary.

FAIRBANKS
MAY 3-5, 1985

The first Friday in May seems a propitious time to journey northward to the Interior on a mission of disposing of house, doing some state-related calling, and seeing my friend Ruth and her boys. So I clutch my ultimate super saver airline ticket firmly in hand and head for the northbound 6:50 a.m. Alaska Airlines flight. This time the Taku taxi to the airport is sound mechanically with no falling shift lever or faulty lights. The driver mentions that the weather was clear earlier and that the overcast would clear in just a few minutes, thereby causing no delay in the departure. After an hour and ten minute wait inside the airplane, while outside visibility is one-half mile and four hundred feet (six hundred feet and one mile are needed to make it safe and legal), and periodic updates from the flight deck along with juice, coffee, rolls, and more coffee, the flight finally gets away from the gate and the runway. A headcount is taken to see how many on board hope to connect with the flight from Anchorage to Fairbanks. As I read the airline magazine slowly - it has to last until Fairbanks - we emerge to blue skies and sunshine and views of the mountain tops that have been successfully avoided on takeoff.

The next impression is that there are no footprints or ski tracks in the snow that remains in untrammeled whiteness on the mountaintops down to the treetops on the green slopes. There are some remote roads or trails at the lower levels and a river winds through a valley as the plane flies toward small coastal islands. As what appears to be a fiord comes into view, the pilot announces that we are at thirty-two thousand feet on the way to thirty-five thousand feet and are ninety-five miles southeast of Yakutat near Glacier Bay and Mount Fairweather. There is some breakup in a wide river of ice snaking through the glaciers. No life is visible over the endless white miles. Omelette at thirty-five thousand feet and more juice and coffee. The on-board facilities may get a workout today. Into Anchorage International back on schedule but Fairbanks bound passengers are let off first to allow connecting with Flight 81 onward. Except that the gate number is not known. The flight is due out at 9:50 a.m. and has not yet boarded. Time for a partial pit stop and then on board. More rolls, juice, and coffee as the flight passes Mt. McKinley aka Denali, then one hundred mile visibility and thirteen miles to the airport at Fairbanks. Right on time after all.

Friend Ruth arrives a few minutes later in her classic 1966 Volvo which has lasted through another Fairbanks winter. We go for coffee and late breakfast and discuss what is happening in our respective spheres. Old friends at ease as she discusses a new person in her life and his concerns about my visit - which are unfounded. After a few downtown errands, I am loaned the Volvo to do my tasks. Meet with a deputy attorney general to discuss cases, see the real estate person about when the house will no longer be mine, visit sister in her new apartment before coaxing the Volvo to Ruth's place. Where I volunteer to do a contemplated roast before I find that her former spouse took most of the kitchen stuff a year earlier and that some improvisations are needed to do the veggies that will surround the roast. Not to worry. New Person In Her Life arrives and the concerns are no longer. The roast is put on low oven status and we head for an art event. Which turns out to be hosted by a man in white coveralls while the room lights are out before he proceeds to use a light stick of blue hue while talking about the particle board outhouse with dome that is the artwork. He is a communicator, not an artist. The outhouse has a dome and is stenciled on each side with the figure of a man with a briefcase. Images are formed by exploding flashbulbs on each wall. What is in the outhouse will be awarded - with the outhouse - to the person who can open the combination lock on the outhouse door. The outhouse has a drain or vent sloping up from the rear wall. The title is "The Fortune Cookie Never Lies". I am baffled.

Contemplation of this "experience" is done while having soft drinks at the pub at the University of Alaska - Fairbanks student union en route to a poetry reading that is scrubbed in favor of touring the Chena Pump House, which is one of the better places in Fairbanks. I had been to the place for brunch but was not aware of how crowded it is on a Friday evening. Which does not affect the goal of shooting pool near the ornate stained glass windows and adjacent mirrors. All of which are the subject of a brass warning sign listing prices levied on errant pool shooters who might damage them. Four games later I have proved that I can make brilliant shots followed by ones that are impossibly bad. Back to the roast which is not yet overdone even after six hours of cooking. The invited pool partners don't show, which is good, as the roast could not have easily served four more people. Talk, play Trivial Pursuit without the board for a while and to rest. Saturday with no errands is a treat, just relax, enjoy a late breakfast of Eggs Pizza style before touring Safeway for potluck supplies. During which time the Volvo develops a flat tire which has to be remedied before proceeding back to the stove area. As in most Alaska communities, there are not very many main routes and New Person Roger drives by and helps avoid the need to hike with the deflated tire to a fixing place. After which he departs promising to bring the sausage for the potluck dish before it is consumed. He does and we all proceed to a festive dinner attended by about two hundred local residents, followed by a speaker from Los Angeles who left the corporate maze to operate a mission in the depths of Los Angeles. Afterwards, the never setting sun, even in May, makes it a surprise when 3 a.m. arrives. Which causes a late start on Sunday as two boys, ages two and five, are returned by their father. The younger finds my rain hat, not needed in sunny Fairbanks, and does a clown act with it. The older takes the line from the fishing reel brought for him from the wilds of Juneau. A quiet day as Roger takes time to put a mining claim partner/friend on a plane to the North Slope for work and then returns with flowers for the lady of the house. Out to Creamers Fields to watch the wild geese in a game refuge by the city limits. On to Arby's where the impression is that McDonald's might have been a better choice, then to a home show to check the latest in log cabins, stained glass, wood stoves, and similar items. Out to the airport for farewells to friends, old and new, and back to Juneau. Where the rain is waiting. Home again.

REUNION
MID-MAY, 1985

The Venerable Ford is back with me in apparent good health after over two months of malaise, which culminated in a month's stay at a local car dealer's fix-it area. During an errand in mid-March, the absence of a reverse mode led to the discovery that only one forward gear range remained. As that was lower than high and higher than low, some use of the car was possible. However the top speed was a noisy forty-five miles an hour, so Valley trips were made at thirty miles an hour to and from. Not wanting to finish off the transmission or to be forever slow in the fast lane, repair prices were solicited. The Downtown 76 station charged $23. to tell me that the transmission needed repair. That I knew. Their quote for fixing it equaled several others, all at $700. And up. Being concerned about spending fifty per cent of the car's possible value on repairs, I shopped. No used transmissions in town. Ship one in from Anchorage or Seattle for $325. Plus freight. Labor to install it would bring the cost up to the local quotes. Putz along hoping the big bang doesn't happen in heavy traffic. Or at least not too far from home. Then a 1969 Ford Wagon was found possibly abandoned. Check ownership, check city, check property owners and prepare to take the salvage. A treasure trove of parts. Until a "450" logo is noted; it won't fit my wagon. More miles at low speed and parking where no reverse is needed; an art in itself. Then take it in for more expert diagnosis. Which again reveals that it is not a matter of adjustment. By then the new car salesman has appeared to offer the deal of a lifetime: a new car or truck, no cash needed and a $2,200 "allowance" on the wagon. So I juggle figures, needs, local miles traveled, and put a sticker over my desk about the options. The lure of chrome and comfort is strong. And of course a credit app would need to be completed which would take more time. So, except for borrowed rides to the Valley and cab rides to church, I relearn to walk to work. Which reintroduces me to the sound of running water in Gold Creek, the pleasure of fresh air, and signs of better health through exercise. But, troubled by the thought of $250. going out for sixty months, I recant and "buy" the Ford by repairing it with a used reconditioned transmission. Then I park it so that the walking can continue. At 4:30 each workday as I walk north on Egan Drive, I note all the Valley-bound cars that whiz by in the frenzy to get the people home to pass the time until they can whiz back in the a.m. Some will park the rig and spend family time; many will simply spend the interim doing more driving.

RITES OF SPRING
MAY 18-20, 1985

The ground shook in Juneau last Friday from a cause other than earthquake or avalanche. An initial tremor was noted at 8 a.m. Friday in the area of the S.O.B. as the sun broke through and state employee multitudes rushed to the windows to see what this rarity looked like. Some of greater years or those who have been more recently "outside" recalled having seen this phenomenon other times in other places. Crowds gathered on downtown streets and traffic stopped on Egan Drive to witness the event, which in Juneau comes on about the same schedule as Halley's Comet, according to local historians. A later earth tremor was noted as state and federal employees left work early to fish, sunbathe, or to see what the Fred Meyer Store looks like on a clear day. The weight of the state employees rushing to the front side of the S.O.B. caused a settling of the building on that side. After two days of the sun's glow, normalcy returned with cloudy skies and light rain on Sunday.

This is the time of the year when the tour boats start their annual migration up the Inside Passage to Juneau carrying loads of dollar-bearing visitors. Some three hundred fifteen arrivals are scheduled for this season. The season is one of the three seasons in Juneau: the others are the legislative season and the January to December rainy season. Boat traffic on the channel has greatly increased as the fishing time arrives, while the homeowners in the Valley and out North Douglas also uncover their power saws and project away. The outdoor season has fully arrived as the last vestiges of cabin fever are retired till winter. Unless one intends to wake up at 5:30 a.m. or earlier, the bedroom windows need to be covered to prevent entry of full daylight at such early hours. Later, the light will never fully be gone allowing sleep only when energy totally runs out.

My Saturday started with having to choose between three possible work parties, leaving my home and car for later attention. Finding no activity at the church at 9 a.m., I went on to the AYH project and spent four hours shoveling gravel for a drain outside the house. Then on to a hike with the singles group up the Perseverance Trail. The trail is a mere 3.5 miles each way with a one thousand foot increase in elevation along the way. It is rated as an easy trail which makes it ideal for a starting hiker. This is one where the footwear and other gear is not as critical as on the more difficult trails. The disconcerting element along the trail is the use of metal-floored bridges over several areas where slides have destroyed the trail proper. After several switchbacks on the first part of the trail, we came to a point overlooking the Silverbow Mine remnants and the sometimes-open mining museum. Small railcars are still on the scene as the exit tunnel is blocked. Scattered buildings, some up, some down, outline what was once a prosperous mining operation. After a further climb, we take the side trail to Ebner Falls, where the height causes the water to charge wildly toward the valley floor. Scenes like the falls could make me into a seeker of similar views in our state. After the descent down the trail, several of the group went on to a painting house party at a member's home. With the work, good food, trivial pursuit playing, a movie on the VCR and midnight making of strawberry/rhubarb pie (made after having to replace the strawberries which somehow disappeared during dinner), 2 a.m. was suddenly realized. Which made the stairs in my house seem a bit steeper as I started the second day of a "quiet" weekend with church, a brunch gathering of friends, later out the road to fish for the ones that were not responding, and the first boot filling of the year as I slipped into the water while trying to save my stuck tackle. Wet socks can be accepted if the boots are drained; an Alaskan accepts that fact with the same ease as leaving the hot tub on Saturday night and standing in forty-five degree weather while drying off. Those in the Lower 48 may not believe that it is just a normal way of life here.

ANCHORAGE AND POINTS SOUTH
MAY 21, 1985

North on a late Tuesday flight to listen to various bidders on a state contract for claims services. Out to the airport by way of Auke Bay where I unload the post office box of the weekly accumulation. Turn the venerable wagon over to the house sharer whose wife arrives from Wisconsin on the northbound flight that I am boarding. An on-time takeoff and clear skies. Nine months here and the first time that Juneau has been visible, coming or going. An Anchorage arrival at 7 p.m. where I find that the terminal driveway is blocked by four lanes of cars whose drivers have entered the terminal to meet passengers. Locate the rental car through the maze and on to downtown and the motel. The sun makes for a mid-day atmosphere, so with co-workers a decision is made to take a drive before dinner to visit a local establishment called the Bird House south of town on the Seward Highway. South out of the Anchorage suburbs and along Turnagain Arm as the tide starts to change. The effect is the exponential equivalent of pulling the plug out of a giant bathtub. We follow the route used by Anchorageites to leave town on Friday toward Homer for fishing or to the Alyeska

Ski Resort in the non-fishing season. The road is famous for becoming crowded with the reverse flow late Sunday. We discuss an accident in ongoing litigation and decide to view the scene at Mile 78.3 which is about forty-eight miles down the road. A chance to form an opinion based on personal viewing rather than the usual dry trooper report. As we head south, the water side of the highway is a panorama of native fishermen scooping for "hooligans", which are smelt elsewhere. Past the railroad siding at Portage where cars are loaded on for the trip through the mountains to Whittier and the port there which was a WW II project to gain access to a seaport usable in winter. After finding the accident scene and forming a curbstone opinion, back north to the turnoff for the Portage Glacier for a look around out there. A grazing moose points her southern aspect toward the car and continues munching through the muskeg. Back toward town with a side trip to the Aleyeska Ski Area, where the lodge is closed so no popcorn or thirst quenchers there. On to the Bird House where the decor is unusual and the bar has tilted. Watch the tourists whistle for the ptarmigan. Back in Anchorage for dinner at 11 p.m. as the sun is setting. Two days of meetings and then a rush to catch the Thursday afternoon flight south. A stop at Cordova where the pass before the landing gives a view of trees and mountaintops on each side of the plane. No time to take a tour of the airport before leaving for Yakutat, which has a rather short runway. The aircraft is in a "palletized formation" so there is no first class section; that is filled with fish. We get snacks plus wine on each leg of the flight which keeps the cabin crew busy on the short hops. Past more of the state's 5,000 glaciers (There are only 6,000 in the world, announces the intercom) including the Malaspina Glacier and Mt. Fairweather and Mt. St. Elias. A glimpse of Valdez as the descent starts toward Juneau. Smoke from a forest fire in British Columbia obscures the landing somewhat. Home again and still time to join in a picnic out at Auk Rec. The pioneers would never believe that so much of Alaska could be seen in one day.

WHOSE BAG WAS IT?
MAY 27, 1985

With the end of school years at son's college and daughter's high school, some plans had to be made for the summer up to the time that they would meet their mother for a trip to Europe. "Take A Teenager To Europe" with her as the travel agent in charge. John solved his summer plans by finding a painting job at his college and opted to meet the tour in London. Kate looked for work in rural Montana. Finding nothing there, she decided to come to Juneau for the two months before the tour. Rather than quickly follow the route of the pioneers by taking Big Sky Airlines to Billings and a larger airplane west, Father and Daughter decided that travel by rail and ship would start the summer off with some degree of adventure. So it was Amtrak from Wolf Point, Montana, to Seattle, overnight with a family there, a tour of the Space Needle, and on to the Columbia for the trip to Juneau. Seventeen and able to take care of herself, mostly. At least the Columbia came in at 6:30 a.m., not 2:30 a.m. as it did when I arrived here. I took lots of pictures as the ship docked and as she walked up the ramp carrying most of her worldly goods. Then I picked up some of her bags and we headed by Ford to Juneau where the bags were all carried in. While breakfast was being started, I ask where she had gotten the new carry-on bag. She replied that it was not hers but the one I had with me for whatever reason. The conclusion was that we had an extra bag and someone somewhere was short one as a result of the confusion at the ferry terminal. When I called the terminal to report the discovery, the clerk's attitude was that I had taken the bag with malicious intent and should return it at once. I declined the order but did leave my name and phone number. And wondered who to report the employee to. While thinking, I checked the bag for any identification. As I removed a pair of green cotton pants, I casually noted what appeared to be the holding end of a revolver. When I lifted it out, I confirmed that it was the end of a .357 Magnum, a very long pistol, a Dirty Harry Special. Being leery of shooting off a toe or other perhaps essential part, I checked to see if it was loaded. And it was; only one empty cylinder. After removing the rounds, I called the passenger agent back. Yes, someone had inquired. I ask if it was usual for someone to carry such a weapon on the ship when there were no bears to shoot, then said I would turn it in downtown on Monday as the troopers and city police had no interest in it. All of which added a bit of memory material about the arrival time.

THE DAYLIGHT SEASON

MAY 28, 1985

As schools close for the year and the rain is lighter and warmer, the longer days seem to draw Alaskans and Juneauites into a continuing whirl of activities not unlike the frenzied swim of spawning fish upstream. It is also the time when children seem to migrate in increasing numbers between Alaska and the Lower 48 at a rate unheard of in earlier years. For one who did not leave Kansas very much until of legal age, except to see the Land of Oz known as Kansas City, Missouri, it is a societal phenomena. Kate came here from Montana by train and boat unchaperoned and enjoying the adventure.

John is working at his college in Minnesota. Later this summer Kate will be off to San Diego to join a parent/youth trip to Europe led by her mother. A friend's daughter will be off to the Lower 48 for a month and a half. Another friend has one off and one arriving. The list goes on as family units are added to or subtracted from for the summer. Weather continues to play a capricious role in the process. Saturday at 4 a.m. is clear as several of us leave the high school after preparing a lengthy banana split for the senior class as they wind up a night of revelry. Now on to the weekend activities.

OUT OF MAY
MAY 30, 1985

I descend the Juneau-Douglas Bridge to where 12th Street intercepts Egan Drive, push the button to summon the "walk" light and cross the bridge off-ramp to a traffic island where I can wait in reasonable safety while the swarm of Valley commuters rush past on their two-minute green cycle. During which time I observe them confined in wheeled steel boxes in a mass migration to non-wheeled boxes where they will spend the day confined. Lemmings of the daylight hours. Those confined in the various boxes seem to show total acceptance; this their weekday due till the day of retirement or earlier release. Then later perhaps on to some other box. The drivers, charged with some control over direction and power setting seem at least raised from a somnambulant state. The passengers appear to be in limbo, somewhere between the last gulp of coffee at home and the first one at the office. Well-dressed, well-decorated matronly ladies ride as if they had endured the daily ritual forever. Conversation seems outlawed, perhaps limited to a few words at each end of the commute and most likely concerning rain, lack of rain, or when it will rain. In winter, the topic may be snow, more snow, and road conditions. Someday the ever-replaceable riders will be replaced with newer models but the beat will go on.

NEW GROWTH
JUNE, 1985

What I see from my kitchen window and as I walk to work along North Douglas Highway is the vitality of the season as the rain forest comes into its' own. Each morning as I enjoy my standup breakfast of juice, English muffin, cereal, and coffee, I look at the world outside my window. The spruce trees have suddenly donned tips of green so verdant that they seem unreal in their brightness. The ferns and other large-leafed plants under the trees seem to have doubled in size overnight. An illusion perhaps, but one in which every plant seems to be rushing to grow as quickly and as much as possible during the brief time allotted. The process seems unhindered by the paucity of sunshine or the excess of moisture. When I open my kitchen window to more fully enjoy the sun on the trees as the rain falls, I realize how much is going on in the galaxy between the window and the trees. From the small no-see-ums to the flies, bees, and mosquitoes it is a busy world out there. The sounds of the birds make me aware of all that is going on and that I must not stay closed in my box: rather reach out and be a part of the action.

PARENTS
JUNE, 1985

After a late-in-the-day discussion of matters financial with the summer resident daughter, I give some thought to the time I left the family home and the way it has been with my fledgling adults. With my parents, it was as if at sundown they departed to their bedroom and pulled the door in behind them. Their daylight hours were by and large devoted to work with Father off at 5:30 a.m. to the Kansas City Terminal Railway Company by bus and streetcar to be a car inspector/wheel knocker and Mother to run the house and everything connected therewith. This was in the era of Radio in the form of a mid-size Stromberg-Carlson set that would even receive shortwave messages. Aunt Elsie, next door, had a Philco with a cabinet shaped like the arches at a latter-day McDonald's. There was never a great deal of conversation with the children, after all, what did they have to say? And not much among the adults except when visitors (mostly relatives or pseudo-relatives due to long family ties) would stop by. Then, there would be hours, even days, spent exchanging the news of what had taken place since the last visit. Much of the talk was of who was sick, who was well, who had died, what was planted in the garden or on the farm and what the results were. A sort of cross-pollenization that added to letter writing, which was the form of communication before a telephone in almost every home with extensive use thereof. The talk did not include much world news and not too much of local happenings unless there was some local scandal brewing at city hall; mainly family fodder to be digested and ruminated on. So the children, after initial greetings, would be off to explore the neighborhood, if in town, or the crick, if in the country, sort of cut loose to pass the time under a hot Kansas/Missouri sun and carrying admonitions not to get dirty, don't go near the water, and stay within calling distance. Did "They" ever know of our expeditions into the woods, or along the abandoned inter-urban railway tracks or down into the city storm sewers, through the many places where education takes place? The communication between adult and non-adult was on sort of a need-to-know basis where each side divulged only what was thought necessary. We younger ones didn't talk about where we swam in the stagnate backwaters of the Missouri River; they didn't tell us who was dying until the event took place. An age of near innocence as opposed to now when so much is known on both sides. Which is not necessarily any progress.

JUNE 6, 1985

A small cruise ship is tied up as I walk to work. The two large ships of Wednesday have reclaimed their passengers and departed north or south during the night. The channel waters are loaded with floating reminders apparently claimed from the shore during high tide. The mountains above Juneau show more green each day as stubborn snow areas slowly melt. An angry driver gives me an international signal as he has to slow his merger into Egan Drive to avoid hitting me in the crosswalk near the Parkshore Condos. The water in Gold Creek runs clear again after a few days of muddy runoff.

No ducks, no fish.

A FRIDAY EVENING
JUNE 7, 1985

A quiet Friday evening as daughter was called to work, thereby giving the wagon a chance to lounge around McDonald's parking lot and eye the younger models that drift through. The 8 p.m. sunshine is drifting through the trees as I open the kitchen window to see why the channel is duller in color. The illusion turns out to be the result of rain silently falling through the sun's glow. I listen to the birds gossiping in the trees while I use the telephone. Then at 9:30 down to the channel in response to rent-a-dog noises at my door. Watch a bald eagle land upstream as it waits for a possible fish dinner. Look down the channel to the two light-festooned cruise ships tied up near Marine Park. The float planes taking the visitors on sundown rides are making short takeoff runs before banking and clearing the bridge. Up the channel past the breadline the setting sun is framed by mountains on each side of the channel, clouds above, a subtle blend of gold, gray, and magenta reflecting off the water. So that is where west is from here. A lifting up of thine eyes time to glory in the works of our sponsor. Then back up to the house reflect on how great it is to be here.

JUNE 18 -19, 1985

A view from the bridge. Three small cabin cruisers headed down channel toward Taku Inlet, a skiff trailing in the wake of one. A white cruise ship tied up by downtown. Two small seaplanes landing to the north, up channel, probably Channel Flying for the glacier tour. High tide and two guys sitting amongst the driftwood logs on the Douglas side. Street people or walkers? Sun glint off the high elevation snow that remains. Out North Douglas to where the rent-a-dogs are poised on the entry platform steps waiting for someone to greet. Sticks over the rail for a while before becoming housebound. A day when the prediction was for 68 degrees. Lunch with the new resident adjuster for one of our claim firms as he is taken on the client rounds by his employer from Anchorage. Thoughts of fishing later if the weather holds. Keep an eye on the Egan Drive flags during the early afternoon. Sweat off a few drops of rain after leaving work, donning five layers of torso cover and boots and jeans and heading toward Auke Bay. Meet visitors from Anchorage, then join up with boat, trailer and tower. Head west in a sixteen-foot skiff to seek halibut but will settle for what there is. Past Coglin Island toward Shelter and Admiralty. Anchor off Admiralty and drop halibut tackle but no action except for one large rock. Talk and enjoy the three hundred sixty degree view of channel toward Lynn Canal, and Icy Passage. Give up and troll off Admiralty for salmon. Whereupon visitor hooks up and all stop, all gear up and motor up to prevent fouling his line. A ten minute fight to land a twenty-two pound twenty-eight inch King. Not a trophy but very credible. Which, except for a few line nudges, is all that happens. Watch whales spout up the channel as we troll. Return at 9:30 to Auke Bay as the daylight starts to end. Load the boat on the trailer, clean the King and on to late pizza at Bullwinkle's in the Valley. How to store the fish for a few days?

BIG FISH, SMALL OVEN
JUNE 18-20, 1985

The fun and adventure of fishing in Alaska does not necessarily stop when the fish is caught; it can last right through the preparation and serving of the catch. That lesson was learned this summer when I escorted home a twenty-two pound King salmon caught off Shelter Island on a trip out of Auke Bay. The excuse for the late afternoon/early evening trip was to introduce a visitor from Anchorage to the world of fishing in Southeast Alaska. Our host, a state employee during his non-fishing time, is a student of the waters off Admiralty Island and Shelter Island where he has hunted, fished, and camped over the past six years. He is also my supervisor during the work day. His sixteen foot Klamath skiff and trailer is kept equipped with tackle and ready to hook onto at the first hint of sunshine in Juneau. With our town's easy access to fishing, we were able to meet shortly after work on a June evening at the Auke Bay Harbor behind DeHart's Store at 5 p.m. We were well on the way toward Admiralty by 5:30 with time for four hours of fishing ahead.

After checking the fathometer and anchoring up off Admiralty where the tackle intended to entice halibut was lowered, we passed the time talking and enjoying the 360 degree view of the channel toward Lynn Canal, Icy Passage and other islands and water scenery. The sun on the mountain slopes reminded each of us why we live in this great state. If the halibut catching had been as great as the scenery, the entire evening might have been spent there. As it was not, we retrieved the tackle and headed toward Shelter Island to troll for salmon. Guest Reid took the starboard side while I tried the port side and our host got the stern and boat controls. We had been underway with the lines out for about ten minutes using herring on the end of rigged flashers and dodgers when something decided to sample Reid's herring. As the immediate consensus, sight unseen, was that it was a King, the motor was shut off and lifted to avoid line tangling. The other lines, having no action, were brought in to avoid confusion while he who had taken the right seat fought to get the fish to come aboard. After a ten minute battle and a wild charge by the King, we were able to land the King as it surfaced and headed into the net being waved in its' path. A fish bonker was applied to calm the King down before bringing it on board. The catch turned out to be a sizable twenty-two pounder some twenty-eight inches in length, not the biggest of the season but very credible. And which, except for a few nudges when we put our tackle back into the water, ended fish catching for the evening. So we watched a distant whale spout as we trolled before returning to Auke Bay at 9:30 as daylight started to fade. We loaded the boat onto the trailer, cleaned the King a bit and headed for late pizza at Bullwinkle's in the Valley.

While eating, our guest opined that as he was taking a 7 a.m. Alaska flight back to Anchorage, he would prefer to leave the fish in Juneau rather than try to make it part of his luggage. Something about packing it in a suitcase did not appeal to him. I agreed to find a suitable spot in my refrigerator and some way to use the King. The decision took about three seconds. I had in mind an upcoming church potluck where the multitudes would need feeding and so was willing to help the fish to an appropriate destination.

That was when the fun of cooking a fish of that magnitude started. Up to some as yet undetermined point in fish size there is really no difficulty in cleaning and cooking the large fish found and often caught in Alaskan waters. All that is needed is muscle, ingenuity, and an attempt at patience as the fish tries to go its' own way during the process. As most of my training in this art was with catfish from the Delta region outside of Stockton, California, and with the results of charter boat fishing off the kelp beds near San Diego and La Jolla, along with some Baja California adventures with marlin and dorado, some wheel reinventing was needed. When I did the initial cleaning at Auke Bay, I found that there is more of a tendency for a large fish to want to float away while being gutted. Chasing the fish into the water can lead to filled boots if the design limits are exceeded. Also, the knife needed to be used with care as the fish bobs up and down. Gutting one's own fingers is not the goal. Four hands makes the job easier if one is so equipped. Then, when that stage is done, there is a bit more effort required to carry a fair-sized fish along with tackle and tackle box up the ramp to the car. The arm strain is worth the effort and will not last more than a few days, but opening the wagon tailgate involves key finding and using along with setting everything down without dropping the fish. Placing everything on the roof of the wagon is a good move, if possible, but leaving the fish up there while driving home is not. I have left the tackle box on top at times but never the catch, so far.

When I got home, the real fun started. Having, for some reason known only to the house builder, no outside hose bib, I escorted the fish into my kitchen for more cleaning. It became apparent quite quickly that a tripod to hang the catch from would have been quite desirable. The sink would only hold two-thirds of the fish at a time. That made it difficult to hold the cavity open for removal of the last bits of interior contents while also using the sink spray attachment to rinse out the opening. I solved the problem by doing the work in sections as the flexible fish was pointed up, down, and sideways. When done, I moved it to the counter and then, with daughter's help, into a large plastic bag to await the next step. At this point my hope was to keep the entire fish, head to tail fin, skin and all, intact to bake whole for the potluck on the following Sunday. Greet the new rector with a skin and all King Salmon. Welcome to Alaska. So I cleared the top shelf of the refrigerator and managed to angle the sacked fish in. The tail section had to be bent a bit in order for the door to close. Two days later a friend told me that I should not have sealed the bag as air needs to circulate around the fish. Otherwise, the fridge gets aromatic along with the fish. So the fish was debagged, rinsed, and put back into the untied bag with the tail now bent in the opposite direction. The attitude of the fish in the refrigerator caused me to realize that while I could bake the fish in my standard size oven, it would have to be done with the door partly open which would tend to make the oven less efficient. That thought process led to a trip to my landlord's restaurant and an arrangement to use space in one of their ovens on Saturday afternoon. I also borrowed a large baking sheet which, with fish installed, would only leave three or four inches hanging over each end. On Saturday, I located my dog-eared copy of Gordon Nelson's "Low

Bush Moose" to review his recipe for baking salmon in foil. The recipe gives excellent directions for doing a six to eight pound fish as I have tried it on numerous occasions. I saw no problem in doubling the recipe as to onion, green pepper, and tomato, all to be sautéed with thyme in butter. I had no problem in placing the fish on the stale bread on the foil or in getting the sautéed vegetables spooned into the cavity. Making the foil fit properly around the fish was done with dispatch and it only required two people to get the assembly to the car and on to the restaurant. The problem came when I found that the available oven was set at 350 degrees, not the desired 450 degrees, and could not be raised for this project. Rapid thoughts about fish size and lower oven setting led to figuring that one and one-half hours later would be a good time to check the results. So, leaving the fish, helpful daughter and I retreated to home, made a copious amount of dill sauce, and at the appointed time returned to probe the fish with a meat thermometer to find out the internal temperature. The reading was not conclusive as the thermometer was defective so we opened the foil a bit and decided that the fish seemed done. That is, it looked "done", being somewhat flaky, so we hauled it home for defoiling. I then tried to remove the stale bread base which was now soaked with fish runoff. That has never been a problem with smaller salmon but this one refused to roll over without potentially falling apart. Handling a hot fish of that size was not the ideal indoor sport for June. I resorted to two commercial-sized spatulas which I slid under the fish and managed to get the bread out a bit at a time. Next, I found a piece of plywood on the landlord's burn pile, covered it with foil, and somehow manage to nudge the fish onto it for further draining and firming up as it cooled. Later in the evening, I decided that the fish should be kept refrigerated even though the open kitchen window was letting in cool 58 degree Juneau night air. With reluctance and a sharp knife, the last eight inches of the fish was detached and a small cookie sheet placed under the fish sections. By now the moving and baking was causing the fish head to lose parts of the lower jaw so that part was supported by a saucer abaft of the sheet as the fish was put to bed on the top shelf again. After assisting at the early church service on Sunday, I got the fish back onto the plywood with a lot of juggling. A piece of bread was used as filling to restore the head and gill area to a somewhat normal height before returning to the church with fish, dill sauce, and decorations for the fish. The next hour was used to apply parsley to the area where the tail and fin were rejoined and around the perimeter of the fish. Lemon and lime slices were applied to the main body section, a green olive installed as an eye, and the final assembly moved to a serving table. There were no leftovers. Now that I know the drill, next time I plan to use a board over the sink while fish cleaning - or rig a tripod, and to bake the fish in two sections so the cut does not show or can be decorated over. To turn the fish over or move it, I plan to use a board or pan on top as in turning a cake on a cooling rack. It is just a matter of finding another, bigger fish to work with........

SUNSHINE FOR A WHILE
JUNE 22, 1985

Sometime around 2 p.m. on a Sunday afternoon I realized that I should be out fishing or hiking. The delay in response to the presence of sunshine may have been the result of prior false alarms when the sun would appear long enough to lure me outside, at which point I would learn that the sun was on one side of the house and rain was on the other. Or the delay may have been due to a somewhat hectic round of weekend events which kept me, venerable Ford, and the daughter on the go. The race to Sunday calm started on a rainy Friday evening before two days of sunshine which was our longest clear spell this year to date. The rain did not slow pre-weekend running to one place for a chart of last Tuesday's fishing area, to Foodland for items to use at two weekend potlucks, to the laundry and to the cleaners, and to the Convention Center where daughter was doing volunteer work at a chili cooking championship. All missions done except no rye bread for the Saturday night potluck project. Up early Saturday to head for Auke Bay where the Malaspina was due at 10:30 bearing a new rector for our church. Stop at Fred M for film, for shoes for daughter, and for the rye bread. The bread is not there either. On to Auke Bay where church members gather to sing, raise a banner of welcome and tailgate on coffee and donuts. A joyous time as photographed by non-English-speaking German tourists. Then on to stops at the Auke Bay Post Office and McDonald's before going to the church to set up chairs and tables for the Sunday potluck. After which the new rector and his dog are shown the beach where the dog gets a first swim in Gastineau Channel. Encounter the housebuilder whose house is blocking the beach access and discuss property lines with him. Then, still minus the rye bread, prepare for the Saturday evening potluck. Then, still minus the rye bread, prepare the fish for the Sunday morning potluck, stuff the results in the fish, and encase the whole thing in foil. Off to the landlord's restaurant to borrow oven space as the package is too long for my oven. Need 450 degrees, find 350 degrees is available so recompute time, which is difficult as the recipe is for a six to eight pound fish, not twenty-two pounds. Try an hour and a half. Back to Foodland for dill sauce makings and to see if any bread has arrived. Ask and find that the rye was given to the butcher for some type of meat display. Buy sourdough instead. On home to make up the dill sauce before going back to the oven place for the fish which seems done. Then home to unwrap the results and drain the juices. On to the evening potluck with the glop and the sourdough bread and a pleasant evening with friends. Home later to play more with the fish and to get it, minus eight inches of tail, into the reefer. Up to head for 7:45 a.m. church service and serve there at, and back home for breakfast and efforts to get the fish back onto its' board. Then to church again to do the final fish decorating with green olive eye, parsley, lemon, and lime. Choir duty at the main service while the fish waits for unveiling. Serve the fish at the potluck, clean up the hall of tables and chairs, home to relax while daughter is off to lunch. Then out to view Juneau from a tract in Douglas that overlooks all the lower condominiums and apartments. Wind up the afternoon with the construction of root beer floats which seems to be an ideal way to accompany the sunshine. And starting of a more detailed writing about the fish, which precedes this writing.

JUNE 27 -28, 1985

Adjusting to living in a non-tropical rainforest such as Southeast Alaska is possible. That is evidenced by the number of reasonably well-adjusted Juneauites who seem to prosper in our sometimes wet atmosphere. And the plant life makes starting growth during this time of the year easy, perhaps in some ratio to the speed with which metal rusts. The effects of four days of sunshine has an overall negative effect, however. I was awake at 4:30 a.m. Thursday by the sun's full rays being beamed into the bedroom. Which indicates that east is somewhat down the channel and north is sort of across the channel - at least where I live. Which may account for not achieving a proper north-south axis yet. Thursday and Friday were days of wishing I could be out among the tourists. A lunch time stroll on Thursday to the area at the foot of Juneau along the waterfront revealed that a lot of early arrivals had the choice spots for suntan seeking. The meeting Thursday evening was delayed while sun was enjoyed. Friday evening was spent indoors watching the bugs outside. So when rain started late Sunday I stood outside and was a bit thankful the sunny spell was over. There is a tendency to overdo while the weather is clear. Such as the two hikes and the slip and fall on the Dan Moller boardwalk trail. Daughter was a witness to that. The mud and slime I collected in the fall was taken home for later laundry time. Also about the time there are two good days, concern starts that the weekend won't be clear. Sun starts mid-week normally and if there are too many days of sunshine in a row it becomes more difficult to accept the rain again. As long as it is perpetually rainy, we don't know any different and therefore accept, i.e. like having a corn and not knowing about corn pads.

THE ROCKET'S RED GLARE
JULY 3 -4, 1985

Having celebrated Independence Day, The Glorious Fourth, many times in many places, I can now state with authority that Juneau does it best. This year's festivities on Thursday were preceded by events that started last weekend and will continue through next Sunday. The Juneau Festival Committee, which works on plans for the celebration year round, has had the portable slammer with Marshall and Can Can Girls on the road for several weeks seeking those citizens who appear in public without a $3.00 festival button. The button is not much help if a $5.00 warrant is bought and served on friend, employer, or the governor.

On Wednesday, two San Diego-based navy ships docked and off-loaded some 650 sailors. Some of them will play softball against the local Coast Guard people; Squids v. Swabies at Sandy Beach in Douglas. At 7 p.m. a benefit was held for Caje Holst, a young cancer sufferer who laments that he can't get into restaurants requiring shoes, being legless. George Kennedy, Denver Pyle, and Patty Duke Aston are the stars present as hosts and as parade marshals. Daughter works at the benefit while I listen to the whoomps of early fireworks being detonated with echoes bouncing off the mountain slopes. From my desk, I watch the Valley traffic stream into town for the midnight fireworks display which will start the Fourth. This is on the third as the sun stays up too long for a fireworks display on the fourth. I brave the traffic at 11 p.m. to retrieve Daughter and return to park the wagon; walking appears the way to go tonight. Cars and trucks are already lined up along Egan Drive as spectators get seats out and prepare for midnight. We walk south on North Douglas to the bridge where we watch fireworks being set off from the tidal flats. Boats, some tied up, some maneuvering, are waiting on the channel for the big event. The crews are having fun with the whistles and horns. We arrive downtown at 11:30 and find space to stand on the downtown ferry terminal pier. The barge from which the fireworks will be fired is being pushed into position across the channel. On the hour the show starts and lasts for an hour while the watchers oh, ah and scream as the multicolored display unfolds. A real spectacular. Then a walk back home with a stop at the Vietnam War Memorial display near the Subport. On the Fourth, the parade started at 11 a.m. at the far end of South Franklin Street and ran for almost two hours. Lots of patriotic displays and also proof that in Alaska, if a person wants to be in a parade, they can. As at the Fairbanks Golden Days a year earlier, local business people, owners of vintage cars, and anyone who wants to can get in on the act. Here, a volunteer marching band proves that forty Alaskans can dress forty different ways while playing a rousing Stars and Stripes Forever. The military - Army, Navy, and Coast Guard - escort the flags and give a vivid reminder of why the celebration. A rousing good time!

PLAYING HOOKIE
JULY 15, 1985

At this time of the year in Southeast, the introductory greeting at the gathering of the office clan on Monday morning is not "How was your weekend?" but more likely "How many did you catch?" Which alludes to the fact that nearly everyone in the area who is of reasonable age (starting to walk and up) is either fishing, thinking about fishing, or is in the presence of someone who is. Male, female, young or old, there is no north or south, no east or west, just one body united in pursuit of whatever is running. And is the reason that I came to take a few hours of the precious reserve of annual leave and thereby play hookie from daily duties for a few hours on Monday.

The weekend prior was Juneau incarnate; rain spells with an Old Faithful regularity, just enough to dampen some outdoor activities but not heavy and constant. That, of course leads to Monday a.m. when the serfs have returned to the tilling of the state paper farm, being a time when the sun emerges as clouds disappear and nature beckons those who are now committed to bread winning. And a comment from my next-up-the-ladder supervisor who had spent the weekend kayaking in the rain that obviously I did not have a catch report as my boat still won't float. Then, to rub it in, he described how the humpies were literally standing in line to be caught at Echo Cove near Berner's Bay out at the end of the road. That led to his strongly suggesting that it would be best for me to take annual leave so that I could try again to catch a fish. And that he was filling out the leave form for me. I protested feebly for a few minutes as I rushed to complete a few essential work tasks before leaving to change clothes and pick up the things that I would need on the expedition. Having at various times left behind some essential item of gear in the rush to the waters, I carefully assembled all the items that I would need rather than risk some chance of leaving anything behind. Echo Cove is 42 miles and one hour out the road and a long way back for any left-behinds. I carefully placed the fishing permit in the tackle box along with a small camera for taking pictures of my catch. I made a sandwich to accompany the license and camera and put it in the box. I set out the rods and reels next to the Juneau tennies. I loaded the car and set out for Gas & Go to feed the car and then over to Western Auto at Grant's Plaza for a pair of Pixie lures, some steel leaders, and a book issued by the Fish and Fur people at the state that tells how many fish I can keep. The Pixie selection was limited due to other people having the same idea as me but earlier. Back to the car to put the stuff in the tackle box, which was not in the car. So that was what I forgot. Again; as one got left on the dock in San Diego a few years ago and was not turned in by whomever found it. Or, as in Fairbanks last July when I remembered to take the tackle box but left it on top of a loaned station wagon. It did not slide off until the first curve in the road, at which time I made an unsafe stop and ran back to retrieve it. The Plano box must be sturdy; it was scratched but still closed when I got to where it was. This year, I did not even get as far as the wagon roof. Back to town, pick it up from the counter, find the net that I had been unable to find earlier, and on out the road. The mountains, now devoid of most of their snow cover, seemed to be etched against the sharp blue of the sky. A picture postcard day, warm, dry, and visibility unlimited. By 12:30 I was trying to thread the wagon through the trees that line the narrow road to the beach at Echo Cove. A four-wheel-drive road most times. Not for big wagons. Then the routine of strapping on the fish knife, putting pliers in the pocket to cut the line with and take hooks out of the fish and me, add a new leader to the line on the Daiwa 2600 mounted on my ancient seven-foot pole and ready to move out. All the time this was taking place, the fishermen already there were making more noise than the ravens as fish were caught. One had a fair-sized humpie that was being cleaned and taken to a fire on the beach for lunch. Then on down the beach to take a position where I could see the fish splashing and diving in an effort to convince me they were there whether I caught any or not. After an hour of trying to see how many times I could cast out an over-sized Pixie without catching anything, I had a lot of casting practice and two fish given to me by other fisher people who either felt sorry for me or had limited out. Then at 2 p.m., July 15, 1985, after a year of fishing effort in Alaska I a) got a strike, b) kept it on the line, and c) managed to land it. The enthusiasm generated led to more dedicated casting and ultimately two more humpies, not including the One That Got Away and a nice starfish that I sent back. Even the legions of horseflies visiting the beach and back of my neck helped me; the efforts brushing them off gave a motion to the line that moved the lure in the manner of a wounded bait fish. So, finally victorious, I retrieved my string of fish from the water, cleaned them, and headed back to town. The picture of the first Alaska catch may not make the cover of Field and Stream but will be a reminder of life outside the office. And next week....

THE GUEST
JULY 20 - AUGUST 7-8, 1985

As each new Alaskan comes to his or her new home and becomes enamored of the state even beyond what was promised by "The Milepost", there emerges a tendency to invite people less fortunate to share in the now-found splendor. Any letter, any phone call includes an offer of shelter, food, fishing when "you get up this way." There is no limit to those that these invitations are extended to; I even offered to welcome my former spouse but believe that the line should be drawn at creditors. And, of course, as these invites are usually sincere in nature, they are sometimes accepted. Which is how, after ten months here, I had my first non-Alaskan visitor since coming to the Last Frontier.

The arrivee was a friend by mail, i.e. a pen pal who, by virtue of that status, I had never met in person. The correspondence had started as I exited California and was the result of a request to republish an article I had written. My reply/consent somewhat startled the requestor as the envelope bore the address of a California attorney and a Juneau postmark. From that emerged a friendship by mail as I settled into life in Alaska. And a suggestion that if vacation time was spent there, I would try to be a suitable host and guide. The curiosity of a desert dweller to see how people live in the Juneau wetlands may been have the reason that the invitation was accepted and why I was at the Juneau airport on a July evening at 9 p.m. Having taken Daughter to work at McDonald's at 7 p.m. and not wanting to drive nine miles back into town and out North Douglas before the arrival time, I drove nine miles anyway out the road to Lena Beach. The thought was to exercise my fishing reel while waiting. Of course, one so occupied does not dress in formal attire; mine was Juneau tennies, jeans, sweatshirt, and my UAJ cap with the paint stains. This attire meets the dress code of the Juneau airport - except that I caught a nice pink salmon before heading for the airport. After I cleaned it on the beach, the thought came to mind that perhaps a newcomer to Alaska would like to see a freshly caught fish. After all, how often is one greeted by a (really) dead fish? So I decided to let the fish come into the airport with me. Not wanting to unduly upset the security people, I did cover the fish with a towel. Of course the small size of the towel did cause the tail of the fish to be exposed as it wiggled while I walked through the airport. When the guest came into the arrival lounge where I and the fish waited, there was an effort to get back onto the plane but the closed door prevented the move. After learning that my guest does not fish, I had pictures taken to record the scene. We headed for town where we waited till midnight and the trip back out to retrieve Daughter from work. Early Sunday, the well-trained Ford headed back to the airport as Daughter headed South to join her mother on a summer trip and then on to church while my guest rested. After a daytime introduction to downtown Juneau, the airport fish became Sunday dinner. The somewhat unusual start to a visit did not hinder the later hikes in the rain, trips to Outer Point and Echo Cove, and otherwise enjoying Juneau. The conclusion was that there were so many things to do locally that going further into the state would be unnecessary. Of course when I give future invitations, I will forget to mention the fish incident and the fact that my cooking added ten pounds to be flown south.

OUTWARD BOUND, MAYBE
AUGUST 7-8, 1985

Travelers who try to leave Juneau sometimes find that it is not always an easy process. As the earthly choices are limited to travel by air or by water, there are "limitations" even during the summer season. Unless the visitor has a boat of appropriate size or is here on a cruise ship, the Alaska Marine Highway System is the choice of the "two, if by sea" set. The northbound ships tend to leave the traveler at Haines or Skagway where there is still a long drive of about six hundred miles to either Anchorage or Fairbanks. The southbound ships take some fifty-six hours to get to Seattle; therefore air travel is the usual choice. Until this week, I had thought that only the winter season ever presented any difficulty in scheduled air line service to the outside. Not so, as a recent guest learned when trying to get to Seattle on the Alaska Airlines evening flight. The plane toward Ketchikan and Seattle had, as the passenger agent told one small munchkin, an "owie." While the baggage handlers stood debating whether loading would be followed by unloading and the pilot looked for airport operations and the mechanics looked for a part that would solve the problem, life in the departure lounge came to a standstill. It is the status called "indefinite delay but not yet cancelled." The alternative of switching the passengers to an earlier flight, which should have left Juneau already but had left Anchorage two and one-half hours late and therefore had not arrived but had made up a few minutes before the Cordova stop but was not yet out of Yakutat, was considered. That alternative would leave only the four Ketchikan passengers to be taken care of as that flight did not stop at Ketchikan. Any headed for Ketchikan that wanted out of Juneau would have to wait a day or so. A traveler who was to connect with a flight from Seattle to the East Coast was out of luck under any of the choices. As the choices were weighed: wait for repairs, wait for the late earlier/later flight, the passenger agent had a more urgent call to make: "Don't bring the baby to the airport. I'll be home to feed it and then come right back here." So, with that problem solved, the waiters settled down to see what the next development would be. At which point my guest, who had been told earlier that ultimate super saver tickets could never be changed, found that was only so when the passenger wanted to change plans. If the airline has a problem, they are more accommodating. So a change to an early morning flight was allowed, which solved the problem of a possible 3 a.m. arrival in Seattle. That led to an effort to retrieve the checked bags. After a long search and no results, the baggage crew was advised that the bags were on the wagon, not on the plane, as they had not loaded the plane and the bag seeker was not among the through passengers. Then back to town to cancel room reservations in Seattle and to tell Seattle friends of the change in plans. Which led to an early a.m. departure where the only delay was in getting through airport security as the metal detector was not working and every passenger had to be checked with a portable machine. Which led to finding more keys, pens, pencils, and belt buckles than with the usual machine. At least the delay allowed a chance to say hello to a friend who works for the airline in the departure lounge; one of the nice things about living in a Juneau-sized place.

REMEMBERING AUGUST 13, 1985

This day came on a Monday in 1984, a fact that will be long remembered by me as that was the day that I had hoped to head north to a new life. Except that the countdown lasted two more days past that time. The kids did get on the road to Montana and Minnesota on time as I tried to wrap up the loose ends that delayed my leaving as planned. Some of the undone loose ends were still undone when I finally left. A year has now raced by in my life. This year, instead of packing, I went fishing for a few hours - for three days in a row, and brought home two or three each day for the freezer-stocking. Such enjoyment sure beats wondering how far it is to the next Denny's restaurant. And, after all, when the good fishing is within minutes of home and work and the past incarnation was within the smog and suburbia of Southern California, I have to believe that this was the right move. At least I can now see the water and the mountains which was not always the case down south. Now it is a life of blueberries and salmon berries growing wild around the house and of walks to work with stops to see how the salmon runs are doing in Salmon Creek and Kowee Creek. Humpies now and Silvers later.

EPILOGUE
AUGUST 20, 1985

It is raining in Juneau tonight just as it did one year ago when I arrived here. I am better rested this year than last and am certainly more comfortable as I think back to the first day here after leaving the car deck of the Columbia at 2:30 a.m. In retrospect, it has taken as it would anyplace, about a year to settle in to a new place, whether on the "Last Frontier" or "Outside." The job which buys the necessaries goes well, albeit at a slower pace than the prior business endeavors. I spend more time fishing and catching fish than before. Some goals have been reached; this book was one. Some have not; two or three other books are next in order, the exercise program is a year behind and the family photos are not yet sorted. A play, not planned, was written, and will be produced next spring. I have taught a class at the University of Alaska, Juneau, made new friends, become a member of the local Episcopal parish family, coped with the transition, and rebuilt support structures. Now, having settled in, learned some of the local basics, including how to de-worm blueberries, become more aware of places locally and in the state (South Naknek, Chicken, Red Devil), it is time to start the next phase:

get a bigger freezer, a smoker, fix the boat, do the Salmon Derby, explore more by-ways such as the Bird Sanctuary on Fish Creek, hunt some perhaps, camp on weekends. The move was the right choice; now it is time to go further with it. While it is possible to imagine living somewhere else, I can't imagine that I would want to. I would want to live here even if it didn't rain.

NORTH BY SOUTHEAST
AN ALASKAN NEE CALIFORNIAN

It has been over a year since I headed my overloaded Ford Wagon, king-sized mattress and hand truck on top, interior crammed with the essentials that were not put into storage or disposed of, north over the Grapevine toward Seattle. From there, I would take the MV Columbia for a move to Juneau in Southeast Alaska after being a Californian, North and South, for nearly twenty-four years. The move was more than a physical relocation; it involved a transition to a new place with no existing support structures at the same time that the kids I had been raising were off to distant schools and also my return to a prior career field.

Now that the newness has ebbed somewhat and I have resolved some of the rites of passage, I am able to be more objective about why here and why not there, and is there any real difference? How has a Kansas native who settled into the reputed Sodom of California after military service adjusted to life in the Land of the Midnight Sun? My reverie was initiated when a co-worker who has never been too far south of Seattle was selected to attend a seminar in San Diego where I had lived half of my California life. The other half was in

Sacramento and in Chico where the children were born. When I heard of the trip I dutifully sketched a map, listed points of interest, and suggested a few of the restaurants that I am fond of. And remembered the life there on Point Loma, The Cotton Patch for dinner, Mission Hills, walking the dog at Dog Beach in Ocean Beach at sunup or sundown, the beauty of the San Diego Back Country up toward Julian. Years of hard work, raising kids, times good and not so good. Situs of the dissolution, the closed law practice, springboard to the North via an interim job in Upland. Two years of freeway jaunts to Los Angeles and San Bernardino for hearings. Flights to Sacramento and back before an improving economy dwindled my foreclosure-related work. Then on to Juneau, not the true Last Frontier at its' grittiest but perhaps as close as I want to be at present.

So, Mr. Expatriate, do you miss California, wish you were back there? Not really, except for friends and favorite places. The particular chapter has been written; there is no desire to add more to it. This is the new draft. The California/Freeway lifestyle seems almost unreal in retrospect. Yet I lived it for all those years without questioning. So many miles to a dinner with friends. Work that involved hours behind the wheel. Now I can drive forty-two miles and I am out of road. If I want to drive further, I can put the car on the ferry to Haines or Skagway and head for the interior. This, of course, is not the only place in Alaska where air or water is the only way in or out or where the road's end is not too distant. Yet I do not feel confined. And we do have our traffic problems for half an hour in the morning and afternoon when the state and federal workers commute eleven miles between Valley homes and town. As a Townie living out on Douglas Island, I beat the system by walking to work and back in good weather. In California, I could not have done so and would have been unwilling to try. People there just don't do things like that as a rule. In Alaska, with the exception of Anchorage and to some extent Fairbanks, city size allows living and working to be closer together. If one chooses to walk or bicycle to work, it is accepted without comment. As Southeast has a rather rainy climate, many people bike or walk as another way to show their appreciation of the good weather that happens along from time to time. (Summer was on Saturday from 2 p.m. to 4 p.m.) (The Rain Festival is from January 1 to December 31.) When the sun shows up, work is put aside and the rush to the outdoors takes priority. It is nice to be able to be at a favorite spot for fishing, hiking, or boating within minutes of home or office. Anyone who has been nourished by the smog in the Los Angeles Basin accepts the rain as a fair trade.

So, how about the people? In many ways they are the same; in some ways vastly different. They seem to be here by choice and therefore accept the weather, cost of living, and the occasional need to chase bears out of the yard. They are more willing to speak to a newcomer and to lend assistance when needed. It is also a matter of feeling more like a member of the community and less like a number. I walk downtown or in the Nugget Mall in the Valley or through the Fred Meyer Everything Store and see people I know; it is common here and much less so in California. Our pace of life here can be as fast as Los Angeles ever was at times, yet overall seems to involve less stress. There are things one can deal with and things beyond human control such as six inches or more of snow in a day or rain every day during January, all thirty-one days. The people also seem to show more interest in local and state government and to participate more in the process. What happens in Barrow impacts here and throughout the state. (The outgoing mayor of Barrow awarded some $15,000,000 in contracts to close associates during his last few days in office.) Our governor's current and ongoing problems are more closely watched by me than ever were the antics of the Governors Brown.

All in all, the transition has gone well. I, who thought that any city smaller than San Diego would be impossible to live in, now find that Juneau fits my goals, needs, and lifestyle at this time in my life. The crucial difference is that I feel less like just another marcher in a passing parade. With a state population just over one-half million, half of whom live in Anchorage aka Los Anchorage, there is more opportunity to become known in the city and the state while still preserving personal privacy and freedom. There seems to be more incentive for personal growth and dream realization. In San Diego, I advised a client/friend on the legal aspects of getting a play into production; here I decided to write one, did it, and will see it produced. The limits on doing seem less than before. Perhaps this feeling of being able to try new things is the result of living in a community that is not immediately part of an adjacent community. You are doing your thing here without worrying that someone in any or all of the adjacent towns is doing the same thing. While Juneau and Fairbanks do have populations equal to many of the communities that form the mega-cities of California, they are separate. When you leave a city here, it is by and large a long haul to the next one of any size. None of the Pomona-Clairmont-Montclair-Upland-Alta Loma-Rancho Cucamonga chain of cities, each with its' own McDonald's, Denny's, and Chicken Colonel. Yet this is not Utopia. We are worried about urban sprawl, the fast food invasion, the high cost of living, a slow real estate market, the drug and alcohol abuse problem. These things are not exclusive to either state.

So, I find that the basic structure of life here is much the same as before, albeit in a more scenic, more rigorous setting. The job takes the same time out of the week, there are Saturday chores and errands, Sunday is church and perhaps time to hike. The time is used much the same as before with some local exceptions and additions. Such as fishing for an hour or two without having to make a major expedition out of it. I am able to enjoy life more constantly because of being closer to most parts of it without having to drive far or battle crowds when I get to a place to recreate.

In the way that a new love can never be the same totally as a former love, California and Alaska are two different spiritual entities. To be Alaskan now does not make me any less a Californian than I was. So, on with the new life while still on speaking terms with the old. It is, in the final analysis, for me, a feeling that after all the moves, there is a sense of coming home rather than just coming to a place to live.

Order Form

Old Red Barn Publishing
P.O. Box 921
Sequim, Washington 98382
360.582.1598

Qty	Item	Price	Total
	The Road North Tales of an Urban Sourdough	19.95 Canada 23.95	
	The Photo Op	19.95 Canada 23.95	
	HABITATIN' FOR HUMANITY	9.95 Canada 12.95	
		Book Total	
		Postage & Handling: 3.95 per book	
		Washington Residents: Please add 8.4% sales Tax	
		Grand Total	

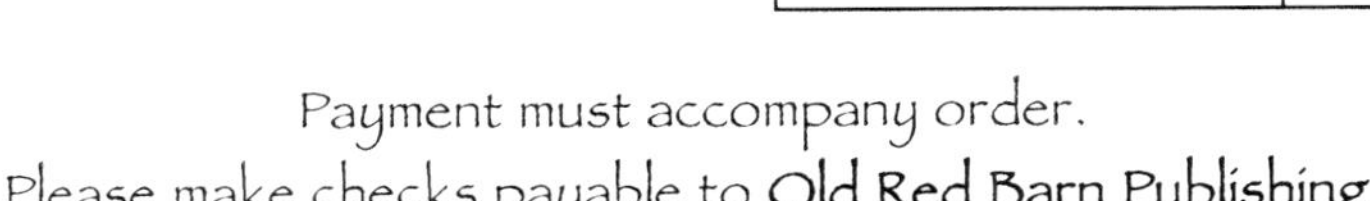

Payment must accompany order.
Please make checks payable to Old Red Barn Publishing.

Name ______________________________

Address ______________________________

City ____________________ State __________ Zip __________

Phone ______________________________